HESS: THE HOLY HISTORY OF ·
OTF

Moses Hess is a major figure in
Zionist thought. *The Holy Hist*
first book-length socialist tract to
synthesis of Judaism and Christi
upon Hess of Spinoza, Herder, a   ..., of Hess' ideas
would find their way into the worl   ...ar x, and into subsequent socialist
thought.

The distinguished political scientist Shlomo Avineri provides the first full
English translation of this text, along with new renditions of *Socialism and
Communism, A Communist Credo*, and *The Consequences of a Revolution of
the Proletariat*. All of the usual reader-friendly series features are provided,
including a chronology, concise introduction, and notes for further reading, in
a work of special relevance to students of politics, modern European history,
and the history of Zionism.

CAMBRIDGE TEXTS IN THE
HISTORY OF POLITICAL THOUGHT

MOSES HESS
The Holy History of Mankind and Other Writings

CAMBRIDGE TEXTS IN THE
HISTORY OF POLITICAL THOUGHT

Series editors

RAYMOND GUESS, *Reader in Philosophy, University of Cambridge*
QUENTIN SKINNER, *Regius Professor of Modern History in the
University of Cambridge*

Cambridge Texts in the History of Political Thought is now firmly established as the major student textbook series in political theory. It aims to make available to students all the most important texts in the history of western political thought, from ancient Greece to the early twentieth century. All the familiar classic texts will be included, but the series seeks at the same time to enlarge the conventional canon by incorporating an extensive range of less well-known works, many of them never before available in a modern English edition. Wherever possible, texts are published in complete and unabridged form, and translations are specially commissioned for the series. Each volume contains a critical introduction together with chronologies, biographical sketches, a guide to further reading, and any necessary glossaries and textual apparatus. When completed the series will aim to offer an outline of the entire evolution of western political thought.

For a list of titles published in the series, please see end of book

MOSES HESS

The Holy History of Mankind and Other Writings

TRANSLATED AND EDITED WITH
AN INTRODUCTION BY
SHLOMO AVINERI
Herbert Samuel Professor of Political Science
The Hebrew University of Jerusalem

CAMBRIDGE
UNIVERSITY PRESS

PUBLISHED BY THE PRESS SYNDICATE OF THE UNIVERSITY OF CAMBRIDGE
The Pitt Building, Trumpington Street, Cambridge, United Kingdom

CAMBRIDGE UNIVERSITY PRESS
The Edinburgh Building, Cambridge, CB2 2RU, UK
40 West 20th Street, New York, NY 10011–4211, USA
477 Williamstown Road, Port Melbourne, VIC 3207, Australia
Ruiz de Alarcón 13, 28014 Madrid, Spain
Dock House, The Waterfront, Cape Town 8001, South Africa

http://www.cambridge.org

First published 2004

Printed in the United Kingdom at the University Press, Cambridge

Typeface Ehrhardt 9.5/12 pt.   *System* LATEX 2$_\varepsilon$ [TB]

A catalogue record for this book is available from the British Library

ISBN 0 521 38347 1 hardback
ISBN 0 521 38756 6 paperback

Contents

The Holy History of Mankind

Contents

Introduction

(1)

Moses Hess is today buried in the cemetery of the first Israeli kibbutz, overlooking the Jordan River and the Sea of Galilee. Yet after he died in Paris in 1875 he was interred in the Jewish cemetery in Deutz, near Cologne, and the epitaph *Vater der Deutschen Sozialdemokratie* (Father of German Social-Democracy) was inscribed on his tombstone; more than eighty years later, his body was transferred to Israel, where he is considered one of the forerunners of Zionism. This is an unusual odyssey for a person who was born in the *Judengasse* in Bonn, became involved in the pre-1848 German radical movement, and spent most of his life as a socialist exile in France.

When Hess is today mentioned in historical studies, he is usually connected with Karl Marx, as both colleague and protagonist in the early communist movement; on the other hand, in Israel he is revered as one of the forerunners of Zionism, since in his *Rome and Jerusalem* (1862), he advocated the establishment of a Jewish commonwealth in Palestine. Yet his writings are little known, and have been hardly translated. At the time, however, he exerted considerable influence, and it was he who introduced Marx – six years his junior – to communist ideas; the latter referred to him, in a somewhat ambivalent comment, as 'my communist rabbi'.

Hess' life story is emblematic of a whole generation of pre-1848 German radical thinkers and activists. Like Marx and Heine, he was born to Jewish parents in the Rhineland, which in the first half of the nineteenth century became the hotbed of radicalism in Germany. The reason for this radicalism was not only that the region was economically the most developed in Germany. At the Congress of Vienna of 1815 the area was annexed to Prussia, but for most of the preceding two decades it had been under French rule – Republican, and then Napoleonic. During this period all feudal privileges were abolished, the French Civil Code was introduced, all religious differences before the law were set aside, and the Jewish population (proportionally larger than in any other region of Germany) was granted equal civil rights. After Napoleon's defeat, the newly established conservative Prussian administration tried to undo much of the French emancipatory legislation: this caused much tension among many of the population, who had grown up under the freer conditions of French rule and, knowing French, had access to French revolutionary literature. This was especially evident among the Jewish population, who found itself once more deprived of civil rights and virtually thrown back into pre-emancipation days. Thus, more than any other area in the German lands, the Rhineland became a breeding ground for revolutionary ideas.

It was into this ambience that Moses Hess was born in 1812 to an orthodox Jewish family of petty merchants. Like many of his background, he rebelled against the constricting education given to him at home and in the traditional Jewish *heder*; though he never attended a German-language *Gymnasium*, he hoped to enrol at the university. In the meantime, he and a group of his friends became avid readers of French and, to a lesser degree, German philosophical and political literature: as Hess mentions in his diaries, his reading included Benjamin Constant and Victor Hugo, Rousseau and Helvetius, Fichte and Goethe, Chateaubriand and Schiller, the medieval mystic Jakob Böhme and the romantic author Jean Paul. It was an eclectic self-education for a young boy whose family hoped he would join the family business; yet Hess wanted to become a writer – though in his diaries he admits his inadequacies:

> A writer? What education did I receive? None. Where did I study? Nowhere. What did I study? It does not matter. I nonetheless became a writer immediately, because I wrote more than I have ever read; hence I thought more than I had food for thought.

It was in this atmosphere of looking for new horizons that Hess came upon Spinoza. To many Jews of his generation, Spinoza was the epitome of the first modern Jew, who transcended the limits of his Jewish background without embracing Christianity: it was a new secular option, just then presented in an historical novel *Spinoza*, published in 1837 by Hess' close friend, Berthold Auerbach. Auerbach, who came from a similar Jewish background to that of Hess, also published a year earlier one of the first pleas for Jewish equal rights, linking this with a general liberalization of political life in the German states.

Spinoza thus became the mainstay of Hess' promise of a reformed intellectual world – and the focus of the first book to be published by him, anonymously, in 1837, *Die heilige Geschichte der Menschheit* ('The Holy History of Mankind). We shall dwell more closely on this work later; suffice it to say that, under the guise of a philosophy of history which views both Jesus and Spinoza as the two poles of a new world order, Hess advocates a radical transformation of society aimed at achieving social equality and the introduction of common property.

The book, published privately by Hess, did not receive much attention, and a few years later, in 1841, Hess published, again anonymously, his second book, *Die Europäische Triarchie* (The European Triarchy), in which he advocates a radical alliance between France ('politics'), England ('industry') and Germany ('philosophy'). Less esoteric in tone, this book brought Hess to the attention of a number of liberal Rhenish industrialists, who were looking for an editor for a new newspaper which they were about to found to advocate liberal reforms in Prussia and Germany in general. On 1 January 1842 Hess became an editor of the *Rheinische Zeitung*. His stewardship of the newspaper – and the newspaper itself – did not last long, and soon afterwards, like many other radicals, Hess left for Paris after being harassed by the Prussian authorities for his views. But the position brought Hess into contact with a wider public as well as with a group of young radical intellectuals and journalists. One of them was Karl Marx, and their life-long relationship started in the editorial offices of the *Rheinische Zeitung*.

It was a crucial meeting for Hess. Though his communist ideas were already well formed from the time of *The Holy History of Mankind*, the encounter with Marx provided him with a wider scope and philosophical foundation for his views. It also electrified him, as can be seen from a letter he wrote to his friend Berthold Auerbach, the author of *Spinoza*:

> Be prepared to meet the greatest, perhaps the only real philosopher living now. When he will appear in public (both in his writings as well as at the university), he will draw the eyes of all Germany upon him . . . He goes beyond Strauss and even beyond Feuerbach . . . Such a man I always wanted to have as my teacher in philosophy. Only now do I feel what an idiot in philosophy have I been. But patience! I will still learn something.

> Dr Marx – this is the name of my idol – is still a very young man, hardly 24 years old; but he will give the final blow to all medieval religion and politics; he combines the deepest philosophical seriousness with a cutting wit. Can you imagine Rousseau, Voltaire, Holbach, Lessing, Heine, and Hegel combined – not thrown together – in one person? If you can – you have Dr Marx.

While written in Hess' customary flamboyant style, this also shows a generosity of spirit on his part: not only was Marx his junior, but at that time had not yet published anything, while Hess had already published two books and a number of articles. Hess' awareness of his inadequate education – which we have noted before – resounds here most clearly, and his deference to Marx, which continued throughout his life, must have had its foundation in this realization.

In exile in Paris Hess moved in the circles of his German radical friends, most of them equally from the Rhineland, many of them of Jewish origin. He was involved in a number of clandestine publications, like the *Deutsch-Französische Jahrbücher* (German-French Yearbooks) and others, in which his, as well as Marx's writings, were published. His articles on 'Sozialismus und Kommunismus', 'Philosophie der Tat' (Philosophy of the Deed), 'Der Sozialismus', 'Über das Geldwesen' (On Money), 'Über die sozialistische Bewegung in Deutschland' (On the Socialist Movement in Germany), 'Kommunistisches Bekenntnis in Fragen und Antworten' (A Communist *Credo*: Questions and Answers), 'Die Folgen einer Revolution des Proletariats' (The Consequences of a Revolution of the Proletariat) served, next to Marx's own writings, as the philosophical foundations of that brand of socialism which later found its expression in *The Communist Manifesto*. Hess helped Marx and Engels in the preparation of *The German Ideology*, and after joining the League of Communists in 1847 also participated in preparing parts of one of the earlier drafts of *The Communist Manifesto*.

Yet for all his close cooperation with Marx, some fundamental differences remain evident. Hess never shared Marx's views that the emergence of ideas ('superstructure') can always be traced to economic and social conditions. While Marx himself occasionally allowed the realm of the spirit some autonomy, Hess remained insistent that spiritual developments have their own, internal dialectics, and cannot be so easily subsumed under economic developments, as usually suggested by Marx.

It is because of this that Hess also maintained that national movements – so crucial in the pre-1848 period as well as during the 1848 Revolution itself – cannot therefore be seen just as epiphenomena of social and class struggle. To him, future liberation would always possess twin aspects – social as well as national. The theoretical basis for this insight Hess found in the Hegelian notion of mediation, and it is thus grounded in a philosophical consideration and is not just a political expression of sympathy for national movements. In an article in the *Kölnische Zeitung* in October 1843, Hess writes:

> Nationality [*Nationalität*] is the individuality of a people. It is this individuality, however, which is the activating element: just as humanity cannot be actual [*wirklich*] without distinct individuals, so it cannot be actual without actual, specific nations and peoples [*Nationen und Volksstämme*]. Like any other being, humanity cannot articulate itself without mediation, it needs the medium of individuality.

This approach is similar to the humanistic, universalistic nationalism of Giuseppe Mazzini, who became, both before and after 1848, close to the circle of Marx – despite fundamental disagreements on the role of nationalism. Yet it is clear why Marx basically viewed Hess as an 'idealist', still stuck in a variant of Young Hegelianism.

In the 1848 Revolution, Hess, like Marx, returned to Germany and there put out in Cologne the *Neue Rheinische Zeitung*. This time, however, it was Marx who was editor-in-chief, and the newspaper was an explicit mouthpiece for a radical revolution, though its communism was sometimes a bit muted.

With the defeat of the Revolution in 1849, both Marx and Hess, like other revolutionaries, had to leave Germany. Marx, after some vicissitudes, found refuge in England, where he stayed for the rest of his life; Hess returned to Paris, similarly staying there until his death.

The failure of the 1848 Revolution caused much soul-searching and re-thinking among the German radicals. Initially, Marx was carried away by the euphoria of the revolution, although in *The Communist Manifesto* he advocated, a mere few weeks before the Revolution's outbreak, a long-term strategy of structural change. Now he became even more convinced that the end of capitalism would come only through a series of internal transformations coupled with patient reforms and organizational work on the part of the socialist movement. Consequently, in the late 1840s and early 1850s he purged the League of Communists of the Blanquist, radical elements who were advocating another attempt at a violent revolution (in the 1870s he followed a similar strategy in the First International against the Bakuninists).

Hess' response to the failure of the Revolution followed a different path. More than Marx he was impressed by the strength of the national ingredient in 1848 ('The Spring of Nations') – in Germany and Italy, as well as in Hungary and the Slavic lands. While Marx and Engels did eventually support Italian and German unification by arguing that only after the national question was solved would the proletariat in those countries be able to focus on class struggle, Hess, like Mazzini, viewed the struggle of oppressed nations for independence as immanent to universal emancipation. He thus supported Italian unification and independence, and viewed French support for it – though politically motivated by French *raison d'état* under Napoleon III – as a continuation of the post-1789 French revolutionary tradition both under Republican and Napoleonic rule.

It was in this context that Hess also shifted his position on the question of Jewish emancipation. As becomes clear in his *Holy History of Mankind*, the Jewish ingredient in both his reading of history as well as his political project is central: universal human liberation will also bring equality to the Jews, and because of the way in which he reads the Jewish contribution to history – through the Mosaic legislation as well as through Spinoza – the Jews bring to world history both a commitment to social justice as well as an existential need for it. Yet it is always within a radically transformed Europe that Hess saw the solution to the so-called 'Jewish Question': the integration of the Jews into a radicalized European culture and society is to Hess the only worthy and achievable goal.

The salience of nationalism in the 1848 revolutions, as well as subsequent developments in Germany, gave Hess pause and caused him to reconsider his position. Hess was the first to discern in German nationalism not only a strong and dangerous chauvinism and general xenophobia, but also the development by German nationalists of a virulent racist approach to the 'Jewish Question': under such conditions, even conversion ceases to be an option. It is a harsh premonition which moves Hess to write in 1862 in *Rome and Jerusalem*:

> The Germans hate less the Jews' religion than they hate their race, they object less to the Jews' particular religion than to their particular noses. Neither religious reform nor baptism, neither Enlightenment nor Emancipation, will open the gates of social life to the Jews . . .

> You cannot reform the Jewish nose, nor can you turn through baptism the dark, curly Jewish hair into blond, nor will any comb ever straighten it.

And in another passage:

> It did not help [the composer Giacommo] Meyerbeer that he was always careful not to include Jewish themes in his operas . . . Whenever mentioning his name, the respectable *Augsburger Allgemeine* adds parenthetically 'actually Meyer Lippman Beer'. It did not help the German patriot [Ludwig] Börne that he Christianized his original name 'Baruch'. He himself admits it, saying that 'whenever my opponents are at a loss for an argument against *Börne*, they always bring up *Baruch*'.

Yet the basic argument in *Rome and Jerusalem* is positive: the Jews are a nation, and like all nations entitled to a polity of their own. Hess always viewed the Jews as a nation, not a mere religious community; but it was only now, under the impact of a heightened nationalism in Europe (and in Germany in particular) that Hess advocated the establishment of a Jewish commonwealth in Palestine – alongside the 'rebirth' of the 'ancient Kingdoms of Egypt and Syria' which would similarly emerge from the dissolution of the 'sick man of Europe', the Ottoman Empire. This, to Hess, was in tune with the general spirit of the age which leads to national, as well as social, emancipation. It is in the context of the ongoing unification of Italy (not yet fully achieved in 1862) that Hess opens his *Rome and Jerusalem* – subtitled *Die letzte Nationalitätenfrage* – The Last Nationality Question – with the following statement:

> With the liberation of the Eternal City on the Tiber begins the liberation of the Eternal City on Mount Moriah; with the renaissance of Italy, begins the renaissance of Judea . . . The Spring of the Nations began with the French Revolution . . . The awakening of the dead has nothing alienating in it in a period in which Greece and Rome are being revived, Poland breathes anew and Hungary sets out to arm itself for the last struggle.

To this Hess adds that, because the Jews maintained a strong communitarian tradition of solidarity, based on the Mosaic legislation which he calls here 'social democratic', the new Jewish commonwealth in the Land of Israel will develop along socialist lines.

While *Rome and Jerusalem* had hardly any impact when it was published – Hess' socialist colleagues viewed it as an aberration, and few Jews cared for such ideas in the 1860s – it was later, after the founding of modern Zionism, to become one of the classics of the Zionist, and especially the socialist Zionist, canon. It has been translated into many languages, from Polish and Russian to Yiddish, Ladino, and Hebrew, and thus eventually emerged as the best known of Hess' writings. It is for this reason that the Labour movement in Israel, under David Ben-Gurion, transferred Hess' remains from Cologne to the kibbutz cemetery on the shores of the Sea of Galilee, which is as close to a mausoleum to socialist Zionism as exists anywhere in Israel.

After publishing *Rome and Jerusalem*, Hess remained active in the socialist movement, and for some time also served as Marx's representative on the Council of the International Workingmen's Association (the 'First International'), since Marx could not freely travel to the Continent. Yet his writing activity diminished, though towards the end of his life he attempted, not very successfully, to compose an ambitious work, *Die dynamische Stofflehre* (The Dynamic Theory of Matter), in which he tried to present an overall dialectical philosophy of matter and movement, aiming to combine Spinoza's pantheism, Hegelian dialectics, and modern evolutionary science. When he died on 6 April 1875, a non-religious ceremony was held in which he was eulogized by representatives of French radical democrats, German socialists, and the German workers in Paris.

(2)

This volume includes Hess' first publication, *The Holy History of Mankind*, and three of his later articles, composed during the height of his socialist literary activity prior to the 1848 Revolution. They represent different stages in the evolution of his thought, yet point, despite their different style, to the same critical thread running through all his writings.

The Holy History of Mankind, published anonymously in 1837, when Hess was twenty-five years old, is also the first full-length socialist tract to appear in Germany. By hiding behind the appellation 'A Young Disciple of Spinoza' (*"Von einem Jünger Spinozas"*), the author sends a double message to his readers. At a time when radical philosophers in Germany viewed themselves mainly as 'Young Hegelians', the reference to Spinoza suggests an alternative intellectual provenance; and by invoking

Spinoza – the first modern Jewish philosopher – Hess also subtly tells those of his readers who may be Jewish that, like the Master of Amsterdam, he may be rooted in the Judaic tradition, but intends also to transcend it.

As the first socialist book in Germany, Hess' tract stands out as an unusual amalgam: an attempt to propose a socialist synthesis of Judaism and Christianity mediated through an original, if not idiosyncratic, reading of Spinoza's pantheism. Its structure is cumbersome, its sometimes eclectic erudition attests to the author's self-taught learning, its language ranges from the poetic to the wooden, combing quasi-prophetic pathos if not bombast with shrewd social and political analysis.

It abounds in mottoes and quotations, mainly biblical, which seem both to ward off the censors with an apparent display of piety, as well to as relate its pronouncements to an older moral tradition. That sometimes those mottoes – as well as the subheadings of the chapters – have very little to do with the substance discussed under them, may only add to the perplexity of the reader and to the neglect which the book has suffered from the general intellectual reading public as well as from scholars dealing with early socialist thought (or, for that matter, the emergence of Zionism). It can easily be shown that many scholars who mention the book in their writings have obviously not taken the trouble to plough through its sometimes foggy and often repetitive prose.

Yet, despite all this, the book possesses a coherent overall structure and leads towards a clear political and ideological message. Its two parts (I: 'The Past as the Foundation of What Would Happen' and II: 'The Future as the Consequence of What Has Happened') clearly divide the book into an historical and a programmatic section, with the political message advocated at the end already determining the construction of the philosophy of history proposed in the first part.

Hess' philosophy of history is developed under the overall influence of Herder and Hegel, though neither writer is mentioned explicitly in this context. It views historical development as determined by a successive march of cultures anchored in specific nations (*Volksgeister*), each drawing on the accumulated heritage of its predecessors and bequeathing its own contribution to historical progress to those following it. As in Hegel, transitions are mediated through the work and acts of world-historical figures; as in Herder, each historical period or nation goes through the three stages of growth, flourishing, and decline (under the impact of some writers on natural sciences, the botanical and biological analogies are more pronounced in Hess than in Herder himself).

Yet while this structure of world-historical development, and its dialectical internal relations and ultimate telos, are typical of early nineteenth-century German intellectual writing, its context is innovative and might even have been disturbing to many of Hess' readers. The conventional reading of world history then prevalent in historical writing in Germany (whose traces can still be discerned even today in many conventional history books) would start with ancient Greece and Rome, perhaps preceded by the Orient (ancient Egypt and Mesopotamia), then move through the Middle Ages towards the modern age. In this structure, the Jews (if mentioned at all) would appear on the margin, as a footnote or an almost irrelevant curiosity; though because of the origins of monotheism and Christianity it would be difficult to disregard them completely. Certainly they would disappear almost completely from any meaningful scheme or periodization of history after the appearance of Jesus or the destruction of the Temple in AD 71.

As already implied in the reference to Spinoza, Hess turns the tables on this marginalization of the Jews in the conventional scheme of history: rather than presenting the pagan-Christian (i.e. Gentile, though Hess never uses the term) component as the central axis of history, with the Jews relegated to the margin, he proposes a philosophy of history which (at least in its headings) is Judeo-centric: it is Abraham, Moses, David, and Ezra – and eventually Spinoza – who are the pivots of history, rather than Pericles, Socrates, Caesar, and Constantine. 'Gentile' history is relegated to the margins, and is drawn into the mainstream of world history only through the mediation of that Jew – Jesus – who bridges the gap between the old particular Jewish covenant and the universality of humanity, and whose message Hess views as central to the progress of humanity. This historical progression is to be further elaborated and truly annunciated by another universalizing Jew – Spinoza. One can imagine both Christian and Jewish readers being uncomfortable – for contradictory reasons – with this unusual reading of history. What also stands out is Hess' clear reference to the Jews as a people and a nation (*Volk* or *Nation*), and not a merely religious community.

Equally discomfiting to both Christian and Jewish readers would be the principle of Hess' periodization of history. Following Joachim of Fiore, Hess views history as divided – in the manner of the Trinity – into three parts: the periods of God the Father, God the Son, and God the Holy Spirit. But having adopted this highly Christian reading of the history of salvation, and following conventional Christian theology in anchoring the beginning of the period of God the Son when 'a child is born to Mary', Hess introduces a highly unusual element by suggesting that the third stage of history ('God as Holy Spirit') begins with 'when our Master [i.e. Spinoza] was born to Jewish parents' in Amsterdam.

But it is not only this unique periodization of history which is peculiar to Hess, but also the content he gives to each period. In the first period of history ('God the Father'), which is basically the history of the Jewish people from its inception to the appearance of Jesus, Hess ostensibly follows the biblical narrative. Yet there is a subtle subtext to the narrative, determined by Hess' political agenda which is to appear only towards the end of the book: it is unorthodox, radical, and subversive, and is basically a socialist reading of the Hebrew Bible.

What characterizes, according to Hess, the Mosaic legislation and the old Jewish commonwealth is an internal unity between the political and the moral. Institutionally this meant that religion was not separated from the state (hence the Hebrew commonwealth was a 'holy kingdom'); polit- ically it meant that moral-religious precepts guided the polity; morally it meant that legislation referred to the inner as well as outer man – hence no alienation; and socially it meant that well-being had to be sought in the here-and-now, and not in the hereafter. Hence the old Hebrew com- monwealth was based on the community of property (*Gütergemeinschaft*), limiting the inheritance of property and periodically redistributing prop- erty so as to achieve permanent mechanisms of equalization, if not total equality. The 'holy history' for Hess starts with a sort of primitive com- munism anchored in the Mosaic legislation.

Yet this proto-socialist commonwealth had to disappear – because of internal dissension, arrogance, and the merely tribal nature of the Mosaic legislation. As Hess shows when discussing the second historical period ('God the Son'), Jesus and Christianity overcame this Jewish particularism and created a universal kingdom of the spirit.

Christianity, however, was not only tainted by the corruption of power, which became evident especially in the late medieval Church (here Hess echoes the conventional Protestant criticism of the Roman Catholic Church and the Papacy). Christian spirituality, in Hess' reading, also meant that the New Testament related solely to the inner man, reli- gion was divorced from politics and – this is the crux of Hess' social and moral criticism of Christianity – 'the Christians never possessed a social order based on God; they never had a holy state or a divine law'. It is for this reason, according to Hess, that Christianity too had to be overcome (*aufgehoben*), while preserving its universal message of salvation; but this salvation had to be re-directed to the here-and-now, to terrestrial, social reality. This to Hess was the contribution of Spinoza's pantheism: it recovered, within a universal framework, the unity of matter and spirit which had characterized the ancient Jewish commonwealth – hence it is the ultimate apex of history, the true dialectical synthesis of Judaism and Christianity, now appearing as a new teaching relating to a modern society formed by the development, across the Atlantic, of commerce and industry, leading towards social equality and the abolition of inheritance: while community of property is explicitly mentioned as a desired goal, this is done in a circumspect language – partly due to considerations of censorship, partly apparently as an expression of Hess' own aversion to violence and his preference for gradualism.

All this is sometimes expressed in Delphic language, overburdened with botanical analogies which obfuscate many of Hess' arguments. But as one progresses from the historical Part I to the programmatic Part II, the explicit social criticism becomes more and more apparent.

Yet Hess approaches his criticism of contemporary conditions gingerly, and it is only slowly that the full range of his radical project becomes apparent. In what is called *An Interlude* between Part I and Part II, he refers to the turmoil and *Zerrissenheit* of his age by exclaiming:

> Men have once again reached the point where they are lost without a compass in a sea of errors, finding themselves in the middle of a Noahite deluge of ideas. Where is the ark, where is deliverance?

He is aware that dramatic changes will occur: he hopes they will happen peacefully, and explicitly wishes to defend himself against the claim that 'we intend to bring about or stir up revolutions' and insists that 'we do not wish to excite blind passions'. He is, however, aware that existing social inequalities, which now appear for the first time in Hess' text as the cause of current unrest, can be overcome either 'by peaceful mediation or by violent strife'. He implores humanity to launch an overall effort both to find out the causes of social inequality as well as to develop programmes to overcome them, because if they 'will not be mediated peacefully – namely through appropriate, new laws – they will in the end turn violently into revolutions'. So, despite the apparently careful language, the revolutionary potential is not overlooked, though it is clearly not advocated.

Yet when Hess moves on to the causes of the current crisis as understood by him, the radicalism of his thinking comes into the open.

To Hess, the root of social evil has been the emergence of inheritable private property. Hess does not attack private property as such, though he commends the community of property: it is the heritability of private property – 'historical right' in the language of contemporary German jurisprudence – which replaces individual effort and initiative by passive, corrupting enjoyment of one's parents' achievements. In an interesting parallel Hess compares the heritability of private property with the idea of inherited chosenness which had corrupted the ancient Israelites. Here as there, one generation's achievement turned into the next generation's unmerited claim of possession, and it does not matter whether the goods thus handed over from one generation to another are spiritual (chosenness) or material (property); and just as the ancient Hebrew nation's chosenness has been transformed and transcended by Jesus into a universal link to the divine, so inheritable private property has to be transcended.

Hess does not propose a detailed plan for this radical transformation of society. Yet he explicitly envisages the need to 'create new states', though he is unclear how this would come about, and his radical vision lacks an operational plan; in this he not different from many of the other early socialists, like the Saint-Simonians and the Proudhonists. His message is sometimes contradictory. On the one hand he maintains that 'it is unnatural and atrocious to wish to abolish suddenly all inequality', yet a few pages later he insists that eventually, in what he calls humanity's 'old age', 'all distinction between "mine" and "thine" can again disappear', and 'the primordial equality has to be mediated through the abolition of the right of inheritance'. On another occasion Hess declared that

> Our era strives towards equality – this cannot be denied; but [does this imply] that it is headed immediately towards the community of property? Let this happen one day in the future, let it be the last goal of ageing mankind.

These 'new states' which will, eventually, be organized on a principle transcending private property, will also be organized as national states: 'states must separate themselves according to their distinct tongues'; Hess quickly adds: 'though all are encompassed in a higher bond and live in harmony'. This gentle aside is, of course, quite radical and revolutionary in a pre-1848 context, and hints towards Hess' insistence that future emancipation be social as well as national: the seeds for his call for an independent, socialist Jewish commonwealth in *Rome and Jerusalem* can already be discerned here.

The language of Hess' call for a society transcending private property, and his insistence that the modernizing trends of commerce and industry lead towards it, owe, of course much to Saint-Simonian ideas, and Hess acknowledges as much. But on one fundamental issue he disagrees with them: while Saint Simon, and even more his followers like d'Enfantin, grounded their socialist vision in Christianity, for Hess Christianity – for all of its centrality in his world-historical scheme – is the cause of modern alienation because it preached a kingdom which is not of this world, and thus left terrestrial reality to the rapaciousness of human passions and private property. It is in the ancient Hebrew commonwealth, and not in Christianity, that Hess anchors his social vision, since under Mosaic legislation 'the Jews did not know the difference between religious and political commandments, between what is due to God and what is due to Caesar'. 'Highest equality', Hess argues, 'cannot emerge directly, as the [Saint] Simonists maintain, from Christianity, that peak of inequality'.

The enemy of a just social order, according to Hess, is not the old feudal aristocracy, whose power – both political and economic – has already been broken both by the French Revolution and the emergence of industry. It is the new 'aristocracy of money', and it is through them that man becomes 'beholden to this money-devil [*Geldteufel*]'.

It is interesting to cull from Hess' sometimes disorganized and meandering account the characteristics he attributes to the rule of the aristocracy of money – and compare them with the language used by Karl Marx and Friedrich Engels in their *Communist Manifesto* ten years later. There is no evidence that, despite their close relations in Paris in the early 1840s, Marx and Engels had ever read *The Holy History of Mankind*; yet Hess repeated many of his ideas in some of his later articles, of which Marx was clearly aware: they also sometimes appeared in collections which he himself edited. Be the intellectual archaeology of these articles characteristic of modern society as they are, and in a general sense they represent the common discourse of the *Zeitgeist* in which many of the socialists operated, the similarities are worth pointing out.

According to Hess, the rule of the aristocracy of money causes the following :

Polarization of society between rich and poorer.
Further pauperization.
The poor have 'neither fatherland nor family'.
Also with the disappearance of the old guilds and corporations, the middle classes and the artisanate are being squeezed out of business and will disappear before the power of large conglomerates.

Hess also believed, however – and here he follows the Saint-Simonians and clearly anticipates the Marxist argument, though his language is less coherent and less doctrinaire – that the emergence of modern industry, while causing the crisis of modern society, is also the key to the emergence of a new world of social justice. The characteristics of this new society are spelt out by Hess in some detail, and the description is again reminiscent of some of Marx's later formulations, both in the *Communist Manifesto* as well as in the earlier 1844 *Economic-Philosophical Manuscripts*.

Hess' future society, which will transcend private property, will develop along the following lines:

Abundance, created by socially controlled industry, will integrate overall social interests, and society will be based on altruism, solidarity and harmony, 'because all interests are interwoven . . . Old contrasts between the low and the high, plebeians and patricians, the poor and the wealthy – this source of all collisions, disturbances, iniquities, and horrors – have all lost their poison'.
Peace will reign in society, both internally and externally.
The distinction between town and country will disappear, as 'villages will adorn themselves with wonderful buildings and cities with inspiring gardens'.
Women will be equal to men, and be given the same education.
Free love will replace the shackles of matrimonial bonds which were always linked to property.
Public education will be freely available to all children.
Society will take care of the health and welfare of the sick and the elderly; with the disappearance of poverty, crime will disappear as well.
Formal law will disappear, with people obeying their internal law which will reflect Spinoza's *amor dei intellectualis*.
The people's sovereignty will be guaranteed by the political structure organized through freely associated communities, subordinated to the

overall supervision of the states; the states, in their turn, will be associated in a universal league of nations.

And finally, with industry guaranteeing abundance, human beings will be able to turn their activities to their highest calling – artistic creativity.

These are the main features of what Hess calls 'The New Jerusalem'. While its elements of solidarity are anchored in the old Jewish commonwealth, its universalistic message has been mediated through the appearance of Jesus and Spinoza. To make clear that he is not reverting to another version of particularistic Jewish messianism, Hess makes clear that it is 'in the heart of Europe [that] the New Jerusalem will be founded' – i.e. not in distant Palestine.

Yet the book ends on a high note with a strange and moving ode to the Jewish people, who have incorporated over generations the divine spirit and who through Moses, Jesus, and Spinoza have, according to Hess, given mankind the ability to move from one stage of history to another. The Jewish 'ancient, holy nation-state [*Volksstaat*] . . . perished long ago, but continues to live until this very day in the feelings of its members'. This nation, Hess continues, 'has been summoned from the very beginning to conquer the world – not like pagan Rome by its force of arms, but through the inner virtue of its people . . . [and] this spirit has already permeated the world'.

It is indeed a strange, if not a bizarre, note which thus ends the first socialist book published in Germany. It is a testimony both to the crisis of modern society on the verge of industrialization as well as to the inner turmoil of a young Jewish intellectual who belonged to that generation which – in the memorable phrase of Isaiah Berlin – taught itself German by reading Hegel and Latin by the study of Spinoza.

We have seen that in his later writings Hess would depart from the quasi-religious language which characterizes – and perhaps mars – *The Holy History of Mankind* and to many readers appears to obfuscate his argument. His later writings focus more on social criticism and political action. While he inspired much of Marx's thinking, he also came closer to the latter's vision of historical development which looked more to social and economic realities and less to the heavy Hegelian emphasis on the Spirit, which so much characterized *The Holy History*. In *Rome and Jerusalem* he also switches from his dream of Jewish integration into a socialist, universalist Europe to a more complex approach: he now advocates Jewish integration into a radicalized world through the establishment of a Jewish commonwealth in Palestine. But the major themes of his first book appear again and again, and are preserved in his later writings; a short excerpt from *Rome and Jerusalem* on Jesus and Spinoza suggests only one aspect of this remarkable continuity.

The three other pieces in this volume come from the period of the mid-1840s, spent by Hess in Paris and Brussels, where he was closely associated with Marx and other German exiles who founded the *Bund der Gerechten* (The League of the Just), which later changed its name to *Bund der Kommunisten* (The League of Communists). Reading these articles suggests how the ideas which eventually became crystallized in *The Communist Manifesto*, written by Marx and Engels for the League, had been germinating for some time among the group of German exiles in Paris and Brussels. While it is obvious that the *Manifesto* owes both its analytical depth as well as rhetorical power to its immediate authors, it represents ideas which had been thrashed out in numerous meetings and previously expressed in other publications – though never in the same forceful manner. Hess' contribution to this is evident from the three articles included here. They also represent three different modes of writings: theoretical, popular, and programmatic.

The first, *Socialism and Communism*, is ostensibly a review of a book written by a Prussian official, Lorenz von Stein, on French revolutionary ideas. Stein, a moderate Hegelian, meant his book as a cautionary tale, warning against the dangers of French-style communist and socialist ideas; yet Hess – like other German authors of the period – uses this book as a way to acquaint readers in Germany with French revolutionary ideas, but also to suggest how incomplete Stein's account of them is. While Hess agrees with Stein about the provenance of French radical social ideas from the general French revolutionary tradition, he shows their affinity with some critical aspects of German idealist philosophy, and points to the immanent tension between the ideas of *Liberté* and *Egalité*, leading necessarily to a critique of private property.

In *A Communist Credo: Questions and Answers* Hess tries his hand at a popular mode of writing; rather than the dense philosophical discourse which has characterized his own previous writings – and as well as that of other German thinkers like Marx, which was aimed at the radicalized German intelligentsia – this is the first attempt by a German radical not to address his intellectual peers but to 'seize the masses'. This mode is a natural outcome of the emergence of the kind of revolutionary socialism which eventually found its expression in the Social Democratic movement, which tried to combine the theoretical insights of radicalized intellectuals with the social and political power of the proletarian masses.

By adopting the quasi-liturgical mode of the catechism, Hess' *Credo* is, in its format and language, the forerunner of many later socialist tracts. One may wonder how effective this was, but the fact that it was reprinted several times in the 1840s must suggest that it had gained some responsiveness. It is difficult, though, not to feel slightly embarrassed by the whiff of a patronizing style which creeps up here and there; apparently, when adopting the ecclesiastical style of a hieratic and hierarchic liturgy, this may be unavoidable. Yet despite these handicaps, Hess manages to convey in relatively simple language some of the more fundamental tenets of the socialist and communist social criticism developed by him in his more theoretical writings. Of special significance is Chapter IV ('Of the Transition to Communist Society'), in which Hess insists that for all its revolutionary ideology, a proletarian revolution should not aim at an abrupt nationalization of all means of production, but rather create economic and political mechanisms which will, over a lengthy process of fundamental transformation, make private property redundant and supplanted by social property. This would also involve the eventual abolition (*Aufhebung*) of the state as a mechanism expressing class hegemony.

On a theoretical level these ideas are further amplified in Hess' 1847 series of articles, *Consequences of a Revolution of the Proletariat*. Of the four articles under this title, only the second has been included here: it is theoretically the most significant. These articles were written at the time of the close cooperation among Hess, Marx, and Engels in the deliberations of the *League of Communists*, and comparing it with the *Communist Manifesto*, written a few months later, suggests the common pool of ideas which inspired the small group of German radicals then in exile in Paris and Brussels. In pointing out that the crisis of modern bourgeois society stems from over-production, that economic crises are thus endemic to capitalist production and hence only a social control of production can bring about the kind of wealth inherent in the productive possibilities of modern industrialization but hampered by private property – in all this Hess appears here at his closest to the ideas eventually to be propagated by the mature Marx. Equally significant is his repeated insistence that the revolutionary transformation should entail a gradual phasing out of private property, not a sudden and total nationalization, which would only bring out chaos and dislocation – a point crucial to the Marxian project of a proletarian revolution.

Like other early socialists – Saint Simon, Fourier, and Proudhon – Hess lacks the conceptual cohesion, intellectual rigour, and dramatic presentation of Marx, who brought to socialist thought what all his predecessors lacked: systematic academic education and an unprecedented sure grounding in philosophy, history, and economics; to this was added a powerful rhetorical gift, sometimes verging on stinging invective. Marx thus superseded his predecessors, and while his sometimes disdainful manner towards them smacks of arrogance and superciliousness, his claim to be in a different league is basically justified. Yet he stood on their shoulders, and without them his opus would in all probability not have been conceived or carried out.

Moses Hess, with his unique blend of biblical zeal and prophetic vision, contributed a distinct ingredient to what was to become the corpus of European socialism. What the moral fervour of his socialist critique lacked in systematic economic analysis was amply compensated for by his sensitivity to human suffering and his innovative thinking on social and national issues. In the pantheon of the minor prophets of European nineteenth-century social thought, he deserves his place.

In his understanding of the centrality of nationalism to modern history Hess was aware of a cultural and intellectual force to which many of his socialist colleagues were almost totally blind. It was this aspect of social life which some schools of socialism – like the Austro-Marxists and in a way Soviet Leninism and Titoism as well – later tried to integrate, not always very successfully, into socialist theory. Hess was the first to realize that an abstract universalism, without cultural mediation, may turn out to be hollow, and thus paved the way for a more nuanced, and less dogmatic, socialist approach to issues of national culture, history, and memory.

Chronology of the life of Moses Hess

1812	Born (21 January) in Bonn, Judengasse 807
1816	Hess' father, David, moves to Cologne, leaving the son with his grandfather, so he could attend an orthodox Jewish school
1825	On the death of his mother, Hess rejoins his father in Cologne, continues his Jewish education and starts working in his father's shop
c.1828	Breaks with his Jewish orthodox environment, moves in radical, Young Hegelian circles in the Rhineland
1837–8	Attends, on an irregular basis, philosophy classes at Bonn University for about two semesters
1837	Publication of the anonymous *Die heilige Geschichte der Menschheit* (The Holy History of Mankind) in Stuttgart
1841	Publication of the equally anonymous *Die europäische Triarchie* (The European Triarchy) in Leipzig; meets Karl Marx
1842	(January to December) Editor of the liberal *Rheinische Zeitung* in Cologne; meets Friedrich Engels
1842 or 1843	Meets Sibylle Pesch, a seamstress from a Catholic working-class family in the Aachen region, his future life companion

1843	Travels to Paris, later to Zurich, as correspondent of the *Rheinische Zeitung*; close contacts in Paris with Marx and Heine
1843–5	Writes a number of articles on communism for radical publications, including the essay 'Über das Geldwesen' (On Money); moves between the Rhineland, Brussels, and Paris
1846	*Kommunistisches Bekenntnis* (A Communist Credo) appears
1847	In Paris and Brussels; publishes a series of articles entitled *Die Folgen einer Revolution des Proletariats* (Consequences of a Revolution of the Proletariat); member, with Marx and Engels, of the League of Communists
1848–9	During the revolutionary period, attempts unsuccessfully to revive the *Rheinische Zeitung*, moves in connection with various revolutionary activities between Paris, Cologne, Geneva, Basle and Strasburg
1850–1	In Geneva, as head of the local branch of the League of Communists
1852	In Liège and Antwerp; Prussian authorities issue a general order of arrest (*Steckbrief*) against him; consequently expelled from Belgium
1853	Finds refuge in France where he stays, more or less continuously, for the rest of his life
1854–9	Starts writing on matters of natural sciences for various publications in France
1858	Joins the Freemasons (Lodge Henri IV de Grand Orient)
1860	Begins his work on *Rom und Jerusalem*
1861	In the wake of a general amnesty in Prussia, returns to the Rhineland; begins correspondence with Heinrich Graetz, the German-Jewish historian
1862	Publication of *Rom und Jerusalem*; begins activity in Ferdinand Lassalle's Allgemeiner Deutscher Arbeiterverband (General German Workers' Association); returns to exile in Paris

1864	Following the reactions to his *Rom und Jerusalem*, publishes *Lettres sur la mission d'Israël* (Letters on the Mission of Israel); becomes Paris correspondent for the German *Der Social-Democrat*
1865	As part of his activity in Jewish affairs, joins the *Alliance Israëlite Universelle* in Paris
1866–7	Translates into French vol. III of *Die Geschichte der Juden* (The History of the Jews) by Graetz and some of his other writings
1868	Begins to write for the Viennese socialist *Arbeiter-Blatt*; in September, represents the Basle and Cologne Sections at the 3rd Congress of the International Workingmen's Association (The First International) in Brussels
1869	Publishes *La Haute Finance et l'Empire* (High Finance and the Empire) in Paris as well as an anti-Bakunin tract *Les Collectivistes et les Communistes*, in which he generally supports Marx's line against Bakunin's Anarchists
1870	Expelled from Paris during the Franco-German War; finds refuge in Brussels
1871	Writes numerous anti-Prussian articles in various radical Belgian publications; with the defeat of France and the abdication of Emperor Napoleon III, returns to Paris in December
1872	Begins work on *Die dynamische Stofflehre* (The Dynamic Theory of Matter)
1875: 6 April	Dies after a stroke; the next day a secular service is held in Paris, attended by French and German socialist groups as well as Polish exiles and Jewish activists
8 April	Buried, according to his will, next to his parents in the Jewish cemetery in Deutz am Rhein, near Cologne
1877	*Die Dynamische Stofflehre* (The Dynamic Theory of Matter) published posthumously by his widow

1961: 9 October   Hess' and his parents' remains are transferred from Germany to Israel at the initiative of the Israel Federation of Labour (*Histadrut*) and re-buried in the cemetery of the first kibbutz in Kinnereth, on the shores of the Sea of Galilee

A note on the text

The translation of *Die heilige Geschichte der Menschheit* is based on the text as published in Moses Hess, *Philosophische und sozialistische Schriften – 1837–1850*, ed. Auguste Cornu and Wolfgang Mönke (Berlin-DDR, 1961). This is the most comprehensive edition of Hess' earlier writings – a full edition of all his writings does not yet exist. While *The Holy History of Mankind* is frequently quoted in numerous works on Hess, it has not been translated in full into any language. Even re-publication in German in full is rare: the best edition of Hess' *Ausgewählte Schriften* by Horst Lademacher (Cologne, 1962), brings less than twenty pages from *The Holy History*. Martin Buber's partial Hebrew translation of *The Holy History* in his two-volume 1954 Hebrew edition of Hess' *Selected Writings* has been helpful in elucidating some especially difficult passages in the text.

Hess' sometimes obscure language and convoluted German syntax do not make the translator's task easy, and some passages may still appear opaque: they are so also in the German original. To facilitate comprehension, I have sometimes broken up Hess lengthy paragraphs into shorter ones, avoided (except in a few cases) his excessive use of italics and kept capitalization to a minimum (as in God, Providence, Nature, Spirit, etc.). I retained Hess' division of his chapters into numbered sections. In cases where Hess' text would have benefited from an additional word or phrase, I inserted these in [ ]. When Hess himself uses brackets, they appear as ( ).

The entire text of the book has been translated, except for a lengthy (four-page) motto which contains excerpts from *Klagen eines Juden* (Lamentations of a Jew), published anonymously in 1836 in Mannheim by

Joel Jacoby, a rather unknown Jewish contemporary author. This verbose and repetitive excerpt, mainly announcing in generalized terms the hopes for a new age, for humanity as well as for the Jews, is not particularly enlightening and does not add to the understanding of Hess' own book. Its main significance probably lies in the fact that Hess chose to quote from a Jewish author.

The Holy History of Mankind abounds in quotations, mainly as mottoes to individual chapters and sections. Most of them are biblical, and I decided to follow the King James Authorized Version in rendering them into English. Hess uses, of course, Luther's German translation of the Bible, and in avoiding a more modern English version the intended archaism of the biblical quotations, as well as their canonical standing, is better preserved. I have also followed the King James Version in the spelling of biblical names. Other names are rendered according to accepted English usage (e.g. Charlemagne for *Karl der Grosse,* etc.).

In most cases, Hess gives the exact reference of the biblical quotation (book, chapter, and verse); in cases where this is incomplete, I have provided the full reference in [ ]. When Hess brings in a biblical quote or paraphrase without mentioning the exact source, this is added in the Notes. In the few cases where Hess includes original Hebrew words from biblical sources in his text, I have maintained them: the purpose of their inclusion, in Hebrew script in a German text, is intentional and part of Hess' overall historical design, and I decided to preserve this, outlandish as it may appear.

As for the non-biblical quotations, I have tried to trace available English translations and use them in the text: the full references to the editions used will be found in the Notes. In a few cases, especially from medieval writers, where an English version could not be traced, I have provided my own translation.

The translation of the other writings included in this volume is also based on the texts as published in the Cornu–Mönke edition, except for the text from *Rome and Jerusalem,* which follows the Lademacher edition of *Ausgewählte Schriften.*

Bibliographical note

Works by Hess

Very few of Hess' writings have been translated into English: *Rom und Jerusalem* is the only book by Hess translated in its entirety. The most recent and best translation appeared as *The Redemption of Israel – Rome and Jerusalem*, trans. Meyer Waxman, Introduction by Melvin Urofsky (University of Nebraska Press, 1995).

Among his socialist articles, only two are easily accessible in English: 'Die Philosophie der Tat' appeared as 'The Philosophy of the Act' in Alfred Fried and Ronald Sanders (eds.), *Socialist Thought* (Garden City, N.Y., 1964); and 'Die letzten Philosophen' appeared as 'The Recent Philosophers' in Lawrence S. Stepelevich (ed.), *The Young Hegelians* (Cambridge, 1982; reprinted, Humanities Press, N.Y., 1997).

A full inventory of Hess' works can be found in Edmund Silberner, *The Works of Moses Hess – An Inventory* (Leiden, 1958).

The best German collections of Hess' works are:

Ausgewählte Schriften, ed. Horst Lademacher (Cologne, 1962)

Jüdische Schriften, ed. Theodor Zlocisti (Berlin, 1905, reprinted New York, 1980)

Philosophische und sozialistische Schriften 1837–1850, ed. Auguste Cornu and Wolfgang Mönke (Berlin-DDR, 1961; expanded edition Vaduz/Liechtenstein, 1980)

Rom und Jerusalem – Die letzte Nationalitätenfrage, ed., with an Epilogue, Theodor Zlocisti (Tel Aviv, 1935)

Sozialistische Aufsätze 1841–1847, ed. Theodor Zlocisti (Berlin, 1921)

Martin Buber edited a two-volume Hebrew translation of Hess' main works (*Ktavim*, Jerusalem, 1954).

Secondary Literature

Avineri, Shlomo, *Moses Hess – Prophet of Communism and Zionism* (New York, 1985)

Berlin, Isaiah, 'The Life and Opinions of Moses Hess', in *Against the Current* (New York, 1980)

Koltun-Fromm, Ken, *Moses Hess and Modern Jewish Identity* (Bloomington and Indianapolis, 2001)

Lukács, Georg, 'Moses Hess and the Problem of Idealist Dialectics', *Telos*, No. 10, Winter 1971 (this is a translation of Lukács' 1926 German article, which is the most serious attempt by a Marxist scholar both to relate Hess to Marx as well as to differentiate between the two)

Schulman, Mary, *Moses Hess – Prophet of Zionism* (New York, 1963)

Weiss, John, *Moses Hess – Utopian Socialist* (Detroit, 1960).

There are chapters devoted to Hess' socialist thought in the following books:

Beckman, Warren, *Marx, the Young Hegelians and the Origins of Radical Theory* (Cambridge, 1999).

Hook, Sidney, *From Hegel to Marx* (new edn, Ann Arbor, 1962)

McLellan, David, *The Young Hegelians and Karl Marx* (London, 1969)

The best and most detailed biography of Hess is Edmund Silberner's *Moses Hess – Geschichte seines Lebens* (Leiden, 1966). Silberner, together with Werner Blumenberg, also edited Hess' correspondence as *Briefwechsel* (The Hague, 1959)

The Holy History of Mankind

By a Young Disciple of Spinoza

And if any man shall take away from the words of the book of this prophecy, God shall take away his part out of the book of life, and out of the holy city, and from the things which are written in this book.

Revelation [22:19]

Stuttgart
Hallberg's Bookstore
1837

I

To all God-fearing governments

Part One
The Past as the Foundation of what would happen

The letter killeth, but the spirit giveth life.

2 CORINTHIANS 3:6

CHAPTER ONE

The First Main Period of the Holy History – or the History of Revelation of God, the Father

And the eyes of them both were opened, and they knew that they were naked; and they sewed fig leaves together, and made themselves aprons.

GENESIS 3:7

Hear, O Israel: The Lord our God is one Lord.

DEUTERONOMY 6:4

First Period: India. From Adam to the Deluge

This is the book of the generations of Adam. In the day that God
created man, in the likeness of God made he him.   Genesis 5:1

(1)

Adam was the last and most noble product of the earth after it stopped
bearing fruit. And the fruit which it brought forth into the world multiplied and became ever more noble, each according to its own art. But
Adam was the kernel of the spirit, which would reach its perfection in his
descendants. His soul was whole; he lived in the Eden of his innocence
and bliss. But the time arrived when he felt a discord within himself, as
ill-balanced passions arose in him, which put him in conflict with his own
self and exiled him from his Eden. So began the apex and the glory of his
life, after which he faced his death. This, however, was caused by love,
which pushed him to seek his spouse. Because man is only half a life, and
his spirit is unfulfilled until he is again united with the woman, which was
in the beginning one with him, but later appeared separated from him.
So when the two spouses found each other, they loved each other. But
in this Adam has not yet recognized the value of life, since he lived without
consciousness and without guilt. Only when he painfully felt the absence
of his life companion, the division in his innermost self, did he strive
relentlessly after his lost bliss and finally recognized his life in the woman.
    This was the beginning of the knowledge of God, who is life. This
was the time when God revealed himself to man for the first time, after
having enjoyed the tree of knowledge. Because when Adam tasted the fruit
which was forbidden to him, he saw more than all the creatures which
had preceded him, and deeper than all those who lived with him, as he
was the unity and the centre of all and was now conscious of himself.
Because when Adam knew his wife, the seed of a new human being was
created in his inner self as well as in the external [world]. And this seed
grew internally, and tore the womb, and the mother gave birth in pain:
but the fruit comforted her for her pain. Later it came to pass that the
mortal garment of the first human couple, after it had borne its fruit and
achieved the knowledge of God to which it was destined, followed the laws
of time by a revolution of nature and returned to [the dust] from which
it had been created. The children of Adam soon split apart, and then got

reunited. But by and large the first human beings lived a life of unity, because they were all still free and equal; therefore they were good and happy and loved each other, and shared joy with the joyful and mourned with the mournful.

(2)

As they multiplied, and their desires grew with their imagination, their unity was transformed into strife, their love into longing and their innocence was lost. Finally, the young species of the Adamites was corrupted by the vices of the old world, whose depravity was enormous. This came to pass when the Adamites began to increase in the land, and daughters were born to them, and men of violence saw the daughters of Adam and how charming they were, and took wives from among them according to their will and fancy. And the Lord said, My spirit shall not always strive with man, for that he also is flesh: yet his days shall be a hundred and twenty years. The Nephilim [=giants] were on earth in those days; and also after that, when the men of violence came in unto the daughters of men, and they bare children to them, [and] the same became mighty men which were of old, men of renown (Genesis 6:1–4).[1] This is how it appeared at a time which was corrupted and deadened in its soul. The corruption of the old world became steadily greater, and it proceeded towards its dissolution. In its womb it carried already the seed of a new [world]; because those of the Adamites were saved, who enjoyed God's grace.

Second Period: Assyria. From Noah to Abraham

These are the generations of Noah: Noah was a just man and perfect in his generations, and Noah walked with God.   Genesis 6:9

---

[1] Hess does indeed follow here the language of Genesis 6:1–4, yet calls 'men of violence' what the biblical text refers to as 'the sons of God'. This is a surprising deviation from what appears to be an unambiguous text, and the only source that could be found for this reading is in the Aramaic Onkolos translation of the Bible, which substitutes 'sons of arrogance' for the original Hebrew 'sons of God'. Hess must have been aware of this gloss, as the Aramaic translation of the Bible was usually taught in the sort of religious Jewish school (*heder*) which Hess attended as a boy.

(3)

And when the appointed time of the old world approached, there occurred the last natural revolution on earth. It appeared as if the deep had broken up, and the windows of heaven were opened, and the deluge stormed in. Thus the old corrupt world went to its grave. But the most excellent of those, who emerged wholesome and cleansed from the deluge and the corruption, was called Noah. He was the man of his age, and in him, just as in his ancestor Adam, the Eternal, who is Life, revealed himself again. And [Noah] saw like him, more than his ancestors and deeper than his contemporaries, because the spirit was [again] united in him. And it was revealed to him that the human race, despite its sinfulness, will never be completely destroyed. Because that is how it is with fleeting life – that while it carries within itself, from its very youth, the seeds of its own corruption, namely its inner strife and death, it also bears within itself the seeds of rejuvenated life through God's eternal grace. Also, a number of laws were revealed to [Noah], which related to the life of society.[2]

(4)

Noah died, and men multiplied once more and were spread over the land. Until then they still had the same language and the same images. Since the tools of language were given to them, they designated the images encountered by them by tones or sounds, and thus language was formed. But the images which they recognized increased from generation to generation. So it came about that as men and their representations multiplied, their language became confused. Because some held these, the others different images or representations, towards which their spirit was inclined; therefore men split apart, despite the external unifying aspects, and each worshipped his own idol.

This was the second affliction of the old world, when men separated themselves from each other and established different associations, tribes, nations, and empires, in which people buried their freedom by giving up

---

[2] This is an opaque yet clear reference to the biblical story of the Covenant (Genesis 9:1–17) in which the survivors of the Deluge take upon themselves the so-called Seven Commandments of the Sons of Noah, which deal mainly with prevention of murder and spilling of blood, and in return God sets up the rainbow as a symbol of his commitment not to destroy the human race. In the Judaic tradition this Noahite Covenant, which is universal and encompasses all of humanity, precedes the later, particular Covenant with Abraham and his descendants.

their equality. The right of property appeared; external inequality followed soon, preceded by the inner, spiritual one. Because with the right of property, the historical or inheritance right had soon to be established; however, with this the door and gate were opened to contingency and arbitrariness, to superstition and blind obedience, to injustice and slavery – because now the achievement of ancestors was passed on to their undeserving descendants.

But in the midst of this great confusion of languages and nations there emerged once again, through the eternal law of time, a man in whose spirit the different images or representations of his contemporaries were brought together. And he saw again, like his great ancestors, more than his [immediate] predecessors, deeper than his contemporaries. For he once again recognized the One who is Life, and honoured Him in spirit and truth.

Third Period: Egypt. From Abraham to Moses

Now the Lord had said unto Abram, Get thee out of thy country, and from thy kindred, and from thy father's house, unto a land that I will shew thee.[3]

Genesis 12:1

(5)

For the third time the Godhead has revealed itself to a chosen one, known by the name Abraham. Him God had set apart from the great mass of idol-worshippers and slaves, and chose him to be the ancestor and chief of a nation, through which the knowledge of God would spread across the world; so that through him the seed of the recognition, which was sown with Adam, would grow into a root out of which the stem, the crown, and the fruit would emerge. But just as in the life of nature, the earlier, lower organisms continue to live next to the later and higher ones, so in the life of mankind, in history, the spirit of earlier, lower stages continues to exist next to the later and higher ones, and thus gives testimony until this very day to the undeniable laws of nature and human history. Abraham begat Isaac, and Isaac begat Jacob, called Israel. Initially, this family lived together and subjected itself to the eternal law of life and trusted in divine Providence.

---

[3] I have retained the language of the Authorized Version ('a land'), though the Hebrew original says 'the land' (*ha-aretz*), as does the German Luther translation quoted by Hess (*dem Lande*).

(6)

But as they began to multiply, a conflict arose among the brothers, the sons of Israel. And Joseph, the noblest son, parted from his family, and became the germ of the Egyptian bondage, because he came to Egypt, became great and respected in the land, and brought his family, with which he became reconciled, to him. And the children of Israel kept their traditional customs, lived apart, were engaged in cattle-breeding, and were initially happy in the country. But as they multiplied and became so numerous that they filled the land, a new ruler emerged in Egypt, for whom the great Joseph was a stranger, and he said to his people: 'Behold, the children of Israel can multiply so much, that they may become a danger for us: for if a war break out, they can join our enemies and leave the country.' (Because the children of Israel were shepherds and nomads and were not bound in any way to the Egyptians, who as peasants even viewed the life of shepherds as an abomination.) 'So let us deal with them cunningly', the king continued, 'so that they will not elude us.'[4] From this time on, the children of Israel were treated as slaves. But as the pressure on the people reached its height, a son was born to Amram,[5] and he was saved from death and slavery.

Fourth Period: Palestine – Phoenicia. From Moses to David

They have turned aside quickly out of the way which I commanded them: they have made them a molten calf, and have worshipped it, and have sacrificed thereunto, and said, These be thy gods, O Israel, which have brought thee up out of the land of Egypt.   Exodus 32:8

(7)

Moses, the son of Amram, so called because of his miraculous rescue, was educated in the Pharaonic court. Later he had to flee the land, because out of noble anger at the oppression of his brethren he killed, in a rash moment, an Egyptian oppressor. After this he tended the flock of his father-in-law Jethro in Midian, to which he had fled. And he led the flock to the plains of Horeb, where a large face shone at him out of a bush. It appeared as if

---

[4] This is a paraphrase of Exodus 1:9–10.
[5] Hess mistakenly writes 'Amron'.

the bush was ablaze in a bright fire, but it was not consumed by the flames. Then the Lord's voice called to him out of the flame, and when he heard the divine call 'Moses! Moses!', he answered: 'Here am I!' [Exodus 3:4] . . . Soon, however, timidity overcame Moses, and he began to despair of his divine vocation. Yet once he recognized the miracles of the Lord in history, as well as in nature, he trusted in the God of his fathers and proclaimed him among his brethren. In the beginning they did not hearken to Moses' words because of too much pettiness and hard oppression. Later, however, they trusted the God of their fathers and followed with awe the inscrutable ways of the eternal Providence. So many signs and miracles took place favourable to the people [of Israel], that its oppressors were filled with fear and trembling. Even the court scholars and magicians, who at first explained everything away and knew how to imitate it, had ultimately to admit that God's finger was visible here. At every plague which overcame the land because of the stiffneckedness of Pharaoh and his servants, the freedom, demanded by the people, was promised to it. Yet once the plague was over, the tyrants broke their word and perjured themselves; until they saw their own destruction before their eyes, and then they could not get rid of the people quickly enough.

The people thus received the Law of God through Moses at Mount Sinai. After that it still wandered for a whole generation in the desert, survived some wars, and suffered many privations until it became ripe to enter the Promised Land, where the revealed word of the fathers was to be fulfilled. But [there it was also to encounter] what Moses, the divine man, prophesied would happen to it if it became unfaithful to the Law – the loss of its unity and equality.

(8)

Moses was not allowed to lead the liberated people into the Promised Land, because due to its roughness and sinfulness [the people] expressed too much mistrust towards him. Because even during the granting of the Law there occurred the scandalous story of the Golden Calf, in which the mortal moment of time revealed itself. This was the inclination towards idol-worship, which continued until the Middle Ages (as will be shown later). The Israelites also showed themselves often as disgruntled and stubborn. Therefore Moses sometimes became sidetracked in his divine work and lost trust and willpower. 'Oh', he once sighed to heaven, 'Have I carried this people under my heart, have I begotten them? Why, Oh Lord, am I called to carry this nation as a mother carries her infant into the land promised to their fathers?'[6] 'Blot me', he called in despair to God on another occasion, 'blot me, I pray thee, out of thy book (of history) which thou hast written!' [Exodus 32:32]. Therefore in the end he had to give up the completion of his great work. He entrusted his office to the loyal Joshua, who grew under his own eyes and was full of the Holy Spirit. This loyal servant of God led the people into the land which Moses was only allowed to see from afar. Fear walked before him, for the inhabitants of the land had heard all that was told about the chosen people. And Jericho, the first fortress, fell under the sound of the trumpets, which Joshua caused to blow according to a divine command. And the people spread its conquests and fought victoriously so long as Joshua and the first judges were alive. Later, however, it split, and fell into sinfulness and bondage. The great pain of the times became evident. Still, from time to time a saviour emerged from the people, who delivered his brethren from sin and bondage as promised by Moses. But at the time when Samuel judged the people, it asked for a visible king and spoke to the father of the prophets: 'Give us a king like the people who surround us'.[7] Because the people became numerous, felt insecure, and believed that its situation would become better under a king, who will once again unite them under his sceptre. This demand has been anticipated in the Law; and Samuel chose, according to the regulations, a man of the people, called Saul. But he then took away the crown from his head when he, the king, became unfaithful to the Law. And he put it on the head of David, the son of Jesse, who already under Saul's reign commanded Israel's hosts.

Fifth Period: Babylonia – Persia. From David to the Exile

And when thy herds and thy flocks multiply . . . and all that thou hast is multiplied; then thine heart be lifted up, and thou forget the Lord thy God, which brought thee forth out of the land of Egypt, from the house of bondage.

Deuteronomy 8:13–14

---

[6] This is a paraphrase of Numbers 11:12. The biblical text, however, evokes the image of a nurturing father, not mother: 'Have I conceived all this people? Have I begotten them, that thou shouldest say unto me, Carry them in thy bosom, as a nursing father beareth the suckling child, unto the land which thou swearest unto their fathers?'

[7] Again, this is a paraphrase, and not an exact quote, of I Samuel 8:5: 'Now make us a king to judge us like all the nations.'

(9)

With King David starts the period of splendour or blossom of the Jewish people, after which its death began. Under David, the kingdom expanded; the people reached its glory, its external esteem. David conquered the citadel of Zion and the city of Jerusalem; and his son Solomon accomplished the building of the Temple, planned by [David]. Now the stock raised by Abraham reached its crown, the word of the ancestors became true – 'for out of Zion shall go forth the law, and the word of the Lord from Jerusalem' [Isaiah 2:3]. Initially, the country fared well under the kings; the wishes of the people were, for a short time, fulfilled. But as well-being increased, and the country enjoyed peace from its enemies, the inner enemy, lust, raised its serpentine head; the Law was abandoned, as prophesied by Moses: the godly man was right in reminding them time and again of the Egyptian bondage. But they had forgotten the great lesson from the school of misfortune and forfeited their possessions like children, who do not yet realize their worth. Therefore God's wrath was visited upon them once more, that great grief of the times. This started right after Solomon, whose connections with foreign lands seduced him to opulence and lust of all kinds; these brought upon the people hard times, so that the majority of the people offered their oath of allegiance to Solomon's son only under strict conditions. Yet he listened to bad advice, rejected any conditions and even threatened to increase the burden. With the impudent arrogance of a young, reckless despot born to the purple, he answered the people: 'My father made your yoke heavy, and I will add to your yoke; my father also chastised you with whips, but I will chastise you with scorpions' [I Kings 12:14].

(10)

So a large part of the people seceded from him, and chose Jeroboam, the son of Nebat,[8] as king. But Rehoboam, the son of Solomon, remained king of only a few tribes, the main one of which was Judah. From then on, the kingdom remained divided into Judah and Israel. The king of Israel, the notorious Jeroboam, seduced the people to worship idols, so that it would remain separated from Judah and it would not occur to it to go thrice a year on a pilgrimage to Jerusalem. (This was, among others, the command of the Law which was aimed at the unity of the nation.)

[8] Hess mistakenly writes 'Nabod'.

From then on, the ground was laid for the decline of the holy state. Because the later kings of Israel, adhering to common politics, also followed in the steps of Jeroboam. At the same time, prophets arose, who made courageous speeches in front of kings and people, loudly proclaimed the Law and told the renegades what their future would be. They prophesied about old times, and their prophecies came true. Israel soon came under the sway of Assyria, and never rose again. Yet Judea held out for some time, and henceforth remained the only stem of the great living tree of the holy history of mankind. This was enunciated by the prophet Isaiah with the words: 'And the remnant that is escaped of the house of Judah shall again take root downward, and bear fruit upward' [Isaiah 37:31]. These prophetic words were addressed to the pious king Hezekiah when Sennacherib, the Assyrian, threatened Judah as well. And another century elapsed before the Babylonian captivity. This time was marred by the long reign of Manasseh, the murderer and idol-worshipper. Under his better successor Josiah, the book of the Law, which has been lost for a long time, was found again. After him, however, Judea lost its independence. Pharao-nechoh put Eliakim, the son of Josiah, on the throne of the Jews in place of his brother, and as a sign of his supremacy changed his name to Jehoiakim.

At that time Nebuchadnezzar, king of Babylon, invaded the country and subjected its king. But the latter then revolted, and the Babylonian king punished him and appointed in turn a number of kings over the subjected yet constantly rebellious land. Finally Nebuchadnezzar came and besieged Jerusalem and burst into the starved city after having laid siege to it for a long time. Afterwards, there came Nebuzar-adan, a servant of the Babylonian king and burned down and destroyed whatever was left and expelled the people to Babylon.

Sixth Period: Greece. From Ezra to Matathias Maccabaeus

So they read in the book in the law of God distinctly, and gave the sense, and caused them to understand the reading.   Nehemiah 8:8

(11)

The decline of the Jewish nation has not yet arrived: it still has not lived itself out. Thus after seventy years, as the time of exile was up, and Cyrus had announced, 'Let all those who wish return to the land in order to rebuild the city and the house of God'[9] – many were found who left Babylon and did not spare any sacrifice and effort to rebuild the Temple. At the time of the Second Temple the Jews were more observant of the Law than during the First, because in the Babylonian exile they had learned the great lesson and had become richer in the knowledge of God.

In this period, extraordinary events happened in the rest of the world. In Persia, the world empire, religion was, as in Judea, re-established by Zoroaster; Athens and Rome became free, and in blossoming Greece three wise men known throughout the world later appeared – Socrates, Plato, Aristotle – who did not remain, as we shall presently see, without influence on the holy state. Here, in the re-established Judea, there was no period of external splendour, as in the times of the kings; rather, it was the time of inner life, the people turned unto itself. Divine service was re-established under Ezra, the priest and scribe. After him Nehemiah, his contemporary and helper, deserves to be mentioned. They expelled everything alien and foreign from the people, cleansed its morals and collected the Holy Scriptures and traditions, which had been completely neglected by the people and had disappeared from its memory. When the Jews hearkened to the word of God, they became shocked by their lengthy oblivion of the divine, and set out to study the Law. Now a High Priest ruled the land, and great Synods or Sanhedrins busied themselves with the exposition of the laws.

(12)

Then there arose on the horizon of the time a danger, which though coming from the outside, threatened the inner life of the Jews – the Law of God – with death and oblivion. Alexander of Macedonia, the pupil of Aristotle, marched out of Greece and conquered the greater part of the old world. And in his victorious wake he subjugated also the Judeans or the Jews. Though he never treated them in a hostile way, it was his friendliness which proved dangerous to the old traditional Law, because just as everywhere else, it was his wish to spread Greek culture and morals here as well. And in fact the Jews were not left alien to this influence. When

---

[9] This is a paraphrase of the proclamation of Cyrus, king of Persia, in Ezra 1:3: 'Who is there among you of all his people, [let] his God be with him, and let him go up to Jerusalem, which is in Judah, and build the house of the Lord God of Israel (he is the God), which is in Jerusalem.' A slightly different version appears in II Chronicles 36:23.

Alexander the Great died, one of his later successors, under whose rule the Jewish land also fell, chose the path of violence for the achievement of his goals. But what had been gained by moderation, the recourse to violence failed to achieve among these manly spirits. Antiochus Epiphanes – this was the name of the tyrant – wished to introduce in his whole empire the same religious rites, so as to facilitate his rule; he also pressed the Jews to forsake their ancient Law, the teachings of the One God, their protector, and accept the cult dictated by him. Then there arose among the Jews a second Abraham, and founded through his tribe the last period of the old holy commonwealth.

Seventh Period: Rome. From Matathias Maccabaeus to Jesus Christ

We will not obey the king's [Antiochus Epiphanes'] words by turning aside from our religion to the right hand or to the left.

I Maccabees 2:22

(13)

These words were spoken by Matathias Maccabaeus to his sons, and he reinforced them with his sword. And when he died, he left his nation a lineage of heroes, whom he most urgently commanded before his death to live and die for Fatherland and Law. And his sons promised it and held their word, and proved themselves worthy of their pious father. Few in numbers, but having great courage, they defended the nation and the Law of God against the overwhelming power of the oppressor and became the saviours in these times of trouble.

(14)

But praiseworthy as was their zeal for the Law, the blind fury and the fantastic hate against everything foreign reached their height among the Jews during these wars and became, on the other hand, detrimental to the true knowledge of God. The outcome has been that since that time the Jews became proud and belligerent, and internal dissension took place among them in the form of sects. Some held fast to the letter of the Law, others sanctioned also later precepts; but neither recognized God in spirit and truth.

And at that time the Romans reached the apex of their greatness; they destroyed Carthage, subjected Greece, and arrived also in Judea. Pompey conquered Jerusalem and deposed the ambitious Aristobulus from the Jewish throne. But Caesar favoured him again, as well as his son, and after him Antipater, an Edomite. But after [Aristobulus] was later murdered just like his patron, Antigonus, a Maccabean, tried to reclaim the throne of his ancestors. But Rome established Herod, the son of Antipater, on the Jewish throne; this offended the Jews, because he was an Edomite. But they had already been sick in body and spirit for a long time, and the hope for a Messiah, who had been promised to them in all times of vicissitudes, became dominant again.

Then a son was born to Mary.

> And the Lord shall be king over all the earth; in that day shall there be one Lord, and his name one. Zechariah 14: 9

End of the Old Holy History

Note

(15)

Whatever is born in time develops in three periods. In the first it germinates, is united-within-itself and lives internally – this is life's root. In the second it drives and pushes, is split and lives externally – this is life's crown. In the third it flourishes, re-unites with itself and matures – this is life's fruit.

Similarly, the history of mankind too has these three periods, as mankind is a living whole. And according to the same laws, and in the same order, in which in a single person the spirit, or its internal history, goes step by step with its body, or its external history, so in the history of mankind external development goes hand in hand with the inner, spiritual one.

In the [previous] text we have presented – according to the sources of the holy tradition, which shows us how the spirit of mankind developed in the first period – the traces of this development, but tried to follow more its external moments. Here, on the other hand, and in the following notes, we shall strive to follow the inner, spiritual development.

Adam was, as we have seen, the kernel of the spirit. The kernel is the first [moment] which forms the individual, its soul, the focus and centre of gravity, which draws to itself everything which belongs to its life. The human individual, whose essence is of spiritual, conscious nature, has also

17

a spiritual kernel, a conscious soul. The first thing which represents the essence of man, his kernel, is a form of the consciousness of life, a dim idea or notion [*Vorstellung*], which enriches itself through other notions, which it draws to itself or accepts; and these, after they have fused with the former, connect with others, etc. etc.

The richer a human individual becomes over time through the absorption of such manifold notions, which are released into the world and come in contact with it and impact on his soul, the more there develops in his own self a contrast or a conflict between those notions which it had already processed into a living whole – which have already become a soul – and those which have not yet been processed or integrated, reside in him still undigested, and disturb his spiritual health, the unity or harmony of his consciousness.

This disturbed peace of the soul, the true original sin suffered by all temporal beings, would have been incurable, if by God's grace a counter-poison had not been offered to it, as to all other [maladies].

(16)

The conflict between notion and notion, the reason why notions can be set one against the other, is caused by the fact that notions are not whole truths, but rather one-sided errors; therefore we say that it is conceivable for various notions to contradict each other, because only truth is whole and cannot contradict itself; but one one-sided error contradicts another, which expresses truth from another angle. But when fantasy has enriched itself to a certain point, then the different imagined pictures develop such features which appear common to all persons, who thus find themselves both in the separate pictures as well as in all of them. The individual returns to himself and becomes united – with the beneficial difference that his current united consciousness, his present soul, is nobler and clearer compared to his earlier, original one.

(17)

Just as this law appears in the single person, so it manifests itself on a larger scale in humanity, seen as a higher individual. History from Adam to Christ shows us that from time to time, when people multiplied and enriched their fantasy and came into conflict with each other, a divine soul appeared, in which the contradictions of the idol-worshippers reconciled themselves through the knowledge of the One God. Adam was the first in whom arose the idea of God, the unique consciousness of life; [and this happened] after he himself, as the only human being, was split, and lost his one, united original consciousness, his bliss. The blissful consciousness of united life, or the knowledge of God, was lost again through the original sin of Adam's descendants; through God's grace it was revealed once more in Noah, a descendant of Seth, in whose lineage the memory of Paradise Lost reproduced itself genetically and traditionally; it was lost once more, according to the eternal law of all that is temporal, in his descendants – and was finally firmly established, through the mediation of the Semites, in one tribe. With the third revelation, the root of fantasy was consummated; the tribe of the holy people started with Abraham and reached down to David. From him down to Maccabaeus the stem expanded into the crown, out of which the fruit of holy fantasy ripened. [But] so long as fantasy has not yet reached its peak, so long as man could still entertain over time notions which were irreconcilable with those of his ancestors, a relapse into the old conflict was not only possible, but – where such notions did appear – real. Yet whenever such a relapse into the old sin of Adam took place, the conflict was harsher, the mental sickness deeper: the people of God [i.e. Israel] offers historical evidence for this. It is natural that in those cases where the soul of the individual has been strengthened through having been enriched by integrating into itself life and consciousness, there the conflict which forms his soul and its notions must be more decisive. The more the people of God developed itself internally, so harsher and more spiteful did it become in relation to other nations; similarly, the stronger it became, a still-divided spirit arose within this people (as within every single individual) in a much starker and hostile way.

(18)

So the holy, manly fantasy, or the history of revelation of God the Father – the root of the Holy Spirit – proceeds constantly forward, according to a general and eternal law of nature, which is reflected in the individual human being just as in the nation, and in it just as in the totality of mankind. Through repeatedly recurring splits or sinfulness, the knowledge of God rose constantly, became ever clearer. The death of an earlier, dimmer life or consciousness turned into the life of a later, clearer one, uniting within itself its opposite as a living whole.

Humanity is, like man, a natural phenomenon; it develops, like every-thing in nature, according to a necessary eternal law. The major evils which overtook the people of God were seven, which corresponded to the same number of goods or fruits that grew out of them. The last evil was the harshest; because it caused the disintegration of the people of God, never to be resurrected as such. Out of its death, a new, higher life was to emerge. The realm of fantasy came to an end, as all human notions or images regarding the life of nature or of God had been exhausted. And the divine soul which appeared now, Jesus Christ, closed the cycle of fantasy by recognizing once more the One Being in general as well as in particular.

But now, once the passive power of the spirit [*Geistesvermögen*], fantasy, which enriches itself through the adoption and adaptation of external images, has reached its height, as no hostile contrast could appear any more, since fantasy has fully formed itself – now there emerged the active power of the spirit, or the inner life [*Gemütsleben*]. In what follows we shall see how the spirit further found its place and its time in the history of mankind, in order to complete its path towards its goal in a holy order. The character of the following period exists in a contrasting way in the present one. Yet with regard to the course of history, we shall discover a similarity between the two, which is that much more significant since both periods are, as already stated, of totally contradictory nature in their own life.

We ask the reader to follow this path with us step by step, and to compare his judgment with ours and draw his conclusion, whether it resembles ours or deviates from it.

CHAPTER TWO

The Second Main Period of the Holy History – or the History of Revelation of God, the Son

Our Father which art in heaven, hallowed be thy name. Thy kingdom come. Thy will be done in earth, as it is in heaven.

MATTHEW 6:9–10

Verily, verily, I say unto you, Except a corn of wheat fall into the ground and die, it abideth alone; but if it die, it bringeth forth much fruit.

JOHN 12:24

First Period: Rome. From Christ to the Migration of the Peoples

For God so loved the world, that he gave his only begotten Son, that whosoever believeth in him should not perish, but have everlasting life.

John 3:16

(19)

When Jesus Christ appeared, Rome held dominion over the ancient world. And the old epoch, the history of revelation of God the Father – or the knowledge of God in images of fantasy, which had ruled the earth until then, but progressed until it became the holy root among the Jewish nation – has now come to its conclusion. With Christ a new epoch has begun, the history of revelation of God the Son, or the knowledge of God in the feelings of the soul. At that stage arrived at by mankind in its progress, its essence had to break out into a wonderful blossoming, into a glorious crown.

As Christ became formed, he integrated in his divine soul the many opinions which reigned in his time[1] into a living whole. And just like his ancient ancestor Adam in his own time, he saw more than his predecessors and deeper than his contemporaries; because he recognized God who is Life. But God revealed himself to him, as mentioned, not merely in images of fantasy, whose root is in the perceptions of the senses or notions, but in the soul, whose root is a feeling of purely spiritual contemplation.

Among the Christians, the quarrel over the meaning of the old Law ceased, because they had recognized God in man. And according to the eternal law of love, the Christians had to share their knowledge of God with the whole world; because they were the blossom of the tree of the spirit. Jesus Christ, the Man-God, appeared at the beginning of the youthful period of mankind, its flowering; and through his death he brought reconciliation to an era of violence. He came forth as a mediator between God the Father – the root of life – and God the Holy Spirit – the fruit of life. His first young disciples, the first Christians, recognized God that is Life, and surrendered to the eternal law of love. And like the Israelites in Egypt, the greater the external pressure, the more they multiplied and expanded.

(20)

Later God guided also the hearts of the rulers to acknowledge the Christian teaching. 'Because when for ten years the well-organized Christian Church, spread throughout the whole Empire and beyond it, was able, under its bishops, archbishops and patriarchs, to withstand the terrible persecution decreed by Diocletian, when much more zeal for martyrdom was evident than for saving one's life, when all virtues gloriously appeared, leading to heroic valour, and even weakness was elevated into virtue; when all the abuses and confusions, which have crept [into life] suddenly gave way, and when out of the ashes of the martyrs, just as in Rome's wars of old out the blood of the legions, there appeared hundredfolds of heroes of faith – then all the people recognized that immeasurable and irrefutable beliefs inspired these communities' (Joh. Müller[2]).

---

[1] As becomes evident from the following sentence, I am reading here 'in seiner Zeit', instead of 'in einer Zeit'.

[2] Hess quotes this from the well-known history book by Johannes von Müller, *Vier und zwanzig Bücher Allgemeiner Geschichte besonders der Europäischen* (Tübingen, 1810), I, pp. 478f.

Christianity had to appear as separate from the state, because truth had not yet triumphed, as the way of the Lord had still to wander in the desert; the Christian Church would now become powerful and influential. [But] as the Christians multiplied and counted Emperors among their [faithful], their meekness turned into arrogance, their love into selfishness, and the spirit of Christ turned away from them, because the floundering spirits of the old world were yet incapable of receiving the new teaching, and started quarrelling over words. It is not told us today in any tradition, but in the spirit of history we may report that God the Son spoke as once God the Father did: 'My spirit will never dwell in a Christian who is merely a pagan Christian or a Jewish Christian [*Heiden- und Judenchrist*], therefore let the days of his life be numbered.'[3]. Because it came to pass that after the new teaching had taken root in the womb of the old time, a new movement appeared on earth among men.

Second Period: France. From Leo the Great to St Gregory

> But as the days of Noe [=Noah] were, so shall also the coming of the Son of man be.
>
> Matthew 24:37

(21)

Just as did floods of water in the time of Noah, there now flowed innumerable hordes out of mountains and caves and overwhelmed Europe and pushed its peoples out of their places of dwelling. We stand in awe before this great movement on earth, when wild masses, resembling raw clumps of meat rather than noble men, appeared like blind forces of nature [bent] on the rejuvenation of Christianity. It was a revolution half-spiritual, half-natural – a mediator of a future, spiritual revolution; it was analogous to the last natural revolution of the earth preceding it, which appeared after the material Adam, just as this appeared after the spiritual one [=Jesus Christ], in order to rejuvenate the old race.

Among those hordes which came over from Asia, a powerful one arose, Attila by name, who called himself the scourge of God; according to tradition, corpses and ruins marked his path. Finally he was defeated

---

[3] The obvious reference is to Genesis 6:3, 'And the Lord said, My spirit shall not always strive with man, for that he also is flesh; yet his days shall be an hundred and twenty years.'

in France by the combined forces of the Goths and the Germans, but was not yet vanquished. Rather, 'he was full of feelings of vengeance due to the lost battle; he marched to Italy. As the city of Aquileia paid for its resistance with a terrible destruction, as nothing was left of Vicenza, Monselice, Pavia and Milan except smouldering ruins, the barbarian hero prepared in his camp on the river Mencio his vengeance against Rome. No Emperor, no legion, no Senate undertook the deliverance of the fatherland, of the old ruler of the world. But Pope Leo took the Episcopal staff and went ahead into the camps of the Huns' (Joh. Müller[4]). Moved by him, Attila departed and died soon afterward. Europe and the Church were liberated from the barbarians who appeared incapable of civilization, of accepting Christianity. And as the flood of the Huns was followed by an ebb, a new, powerful race [*Geschlecht*] appeared, and took the new learning into its virginal bosom. The knowledge of God gathered strength in the land due to the influence of the great need. In the Orient, which was untouched by it, it had fallen sick and later went to its grave with the empire.

(22)

The times after Leo were marked by constantly continuing storms of barbaric, but also Christian nations, who, in the wake of the [great] migration of people, founded new states. The flood of people [*Völkerflut*], which is for us like the flood of Noah, flows with these times, when new empires were founded; and it supplies us with a picture of the chaos of languages and peoples which followed Noah more than just the mere analogy of floods of water and nations. Because the periods of the Christian era are not so much of material nature as those of the old [world], since their character is more spiritual. Nonetheless we discover an undeniable similarity between them, which becomes even more astounding the more we move forward in history.

In this second period of Christian affliction, just as in the first one, the ground was laid, or rather renewed, for that inequality among men which reached its apex in the Middle Ages. The feudal system draws its origins from these times, as nations once again fell apart, and entered into social bonds which rather than develop into the despotisms, republics,

[4] Müller, *Allgemeine Geschichte*, I, pp. 530ff.

and hierarchies of old, grew into that many-headed monster of social order or disorder which we are used to call the knightly or fief system; it is out of this that in later times were formed the medieval aristocratic-monarchical military institutions, which replaced the old democratic-hierarchical popular constitutions. But in the midst of these confusions there arose a man, who laid the foundations of the later world dominion of the Church.

Third Period: England. From St Gregory to Charles Martell

And He sent unto them Prophets as bearers of good tidings and warners, and revealed therewith the Scripture with the truth that it might judge between mankind that wherein they differed. And only those unto whom the Scripture was given differed concerning it, after clear proof had come to them, through hatred of one another. And He by His will guided those who believe unto the truth of that concerning which they differed.   Koran, Sura II, The Cow[5]

(23)

With Gregory, the Saint, there appears the stem of the Church. He was the only Saint to sit on the throne of the Apostles. Because he humbled himself, he was raised up high by Providence. He was the moral foundation of the Church's sovereignty, just as that worthy ancestor of the Jews [=Abraham] was the absolute foundation of the holy state. Even before he became Pope, he wanted to leave his house and court in order to gain victory for Christianity. But when Gregory was elevated to the papacy against his will, he never tired of spreading the learning of God or restoring it where it was damaged by the wildness of the time. He sent emissaries to England to spread the Gospel; from there St Boniface and many other great missionaries set forth later to bring the Gospel to the nations which were called by Providence to develop the learning of Christ and to bear its fruit. But another great plight had to be overcome, and only after it had been surmounted could Christianity gain the ground on which the apex

---

[5] *The Glorious Koran*, trans. Marmaduke Picktall, new edition (New York, 1992), p. 51.

of its power would grow, reaching its unlimited dominion over the souls [of men].

(24)

It came to pass at that time that in Arabia a son was born from a Jewish mother to Abdallah, a descendant of Ishmael.[6] He was Muhammet, who was destined by Providence to found the mighty empire of the caliphs. As he became familiar with the many and different opinions of his time and surroundings – pagan, Jewish, and Christian – he united the various views in his spirit into a living whole, and founded a new teaching of God. This learning was a premature fruit, brought forth by an early mating [*Begattung*] of the existing religions in the warm fantasy of a man of the Orient.

For the teaching of Muhammet was not higher than that of Christ, but its opposite – just as woman is the opposite of man. It was the passive mental capacity, the fantasy or the materialism of an Oriental, which was revealed in this learning – in contrast to Christianity, in which, as said, the active mental capacity, the life of the mind or the spiritualism of the Occident, made itself known. The sexes began to develop: just as out of Judaism, the masculine principle, Christianity developed, so out of paganism, the female principle, Muhammetanism sprang forth. This fruit of a warm climate ripened quickly. It was like a hothouse plant: within one century it grew into a mighty tree, whose crown overshadowed many lands in the East and the South. And in the year seven-hundred-and-thirty-one of the Christian era, Abdor-Rahman led an army across the Pyrenees and won many battles. He intended to subject all of Europe to the Muhammetan teaching, and filled all Christendom with fear. Then Charles Martell gathered an army of Frankish and German fighters and encamped in the Plains of Poitiers. For six days, we read in the histories, Charles sustained the unequal battle against the trained hordes of horsemen and archers from the Orient. Yet on the seventh day, when the foot soldiers clashed with each other, in a few moments the noble race of the Germans annihilated with an iron arm and bold breast the Arabian army.

---

[6] There is no reference in any koranic, historical, or scholarly source for maintaining that Mohammed's mother was Jewish, and no source could be found for this rather astounding claim by Hess.

Fourth Period: Saxons, Slavs, and Scandinavians. From Charles Martell to Gregory the Seventh

To Carl, the great and peace-making Emperor of Rome, crowned by
God – life and victory!   'German History'[7]

(25)

As the third plight of the Church was over, it proceeded unhindered
towards its apogee. It was through the son of Charles Martell, Pipin the
Short, that the Head of the Church gained the ground upon which the
Church flourished to become the formidable tree which could reach out
towards world dominion. It was at this time that there broke out within
Christianity that conflict about iconoclasm which we consider – analogous
to the story of the Golden Calf – to be the source of death of that period.
Because it bore witness to the yet unsuppressed sway of fantasy, which
still fought against the mind and contested it (as we have shown earlier).

Yet by the time that Leo the Third sat on the Apostolic See, an uproar
occurred in Rome against the Pope, because he had sent the city's flag and
the keys of Peter's Tomb to Charles, the son of the said Pipin, and thus
put an end to the supreme power of the Greek [i.e. Byzantine] Emperor.
He escaped the uproar and fled to Paterborn to his friend Charlemagne.
The latter received him with all due honours and offered him an escort
for safe travel home, yet next year proceeded to Rome himself and sat
in judgment on the enemies of the new reign. And on Christmas Day
of the year eight-hundred of the Christian era, after offering Mass in
Peter's Church, the Pope put a magnificent crown on Charles' head. And
a unanimous cry came forth from the mouth of the people: 'To Carl, the
great and peace-making Emperor of Rome, crowned by God – life and
victory!'

(26)

Thus the extinct Western Roman Empire was restored by Christians.
Charles subjected the Occident to his sceptre and to Christianity: under
him Germany and France were united, and through unity Christian
Europe went from strength to strength. Spiritual and secular power still

---

[7] Müller, *Allgemeine Geschichte*, II, p. 99.

lived in peace with each other; the naked power of temporal lords and the false cunning of the spiritual ones were still subjected to a strict law. But after Charles' death the Empire disintegrated and Christianity fell into schism and sinfulness. Christendom experienced uninterrupted quarrels, and the See of the Apostles was defiled by wicked priests. The great plight of the period broke out. Finally, the Roman imperial crown went to the head of Otto, the great German king, so that henceforward the German king was also Roman emperor. But unity had not yet been established through this; Church and Empire, Pope and Emperor confronted each other as enemies. The German king claimed supreme stewardship over Pope and Church, until a man ascended the See of the Apostles, who restored to the Church the glory and the power and the splendour.

Fifth Period: Prussia. From Gregory the Seventh to the Exile [of the Papacy]

When the grievances and lamentations reach the highest judge in heaven, and are considered by Him, He will dispatch His rod at the transgressors of His commandments; and He will deliver them into the arbitrary power of their enemies, who will say: how much longer should we suffer these rapacious wolves in our midst?

St Hildegard[8]

(27)

The man of the period appeared in the person of the seventh Gregory, who even as cardinal performed important services for the Church. As he became Pope, he bestowed it with respect, that invisible magical power which today we can hardly comprehend. 'His planned zeal, guided by the highest prudence and not less by unequalled audacity and perseverance, had, according to the spirit of the time, an uninterrupted impact on that brilliant position for a whole generation – he had to change the conditions of the whole world' (Raumer).[9] Now began the glorious period of the Church, in which it ruled the world. Gregory the Great laid the

---

[8] Hildegard von Bingen, *Liber divinorum operum simplicis hominis*, in *Patrologia*, ed. J. P. Migne (Paris, 1855), vol. 197, p. 1017 (my translation).
[9] F. von Raumer, *Geschichte der Hohenstaufen und ihrer Zeit* (Leipzig, 1823), I, p. 27.

foundation stone for this world dominion of the Church. Spirituality now formed a closed, firm bond, and spiritual power triumphed completely over the temporal one, [just as] the Pope triumphed over the Emperor.

At the same time the knightly and feudal system began its ascendancy towards it apex, as the law lay low; everybody strove to get as high as his wild spirit drove him. Christian religion went hand in hand with this untamed striving. The divine spirit of Christ had liberated mankind from the bonds of the old law, but did not give it a new one. Thus was the will of God. If mankind was not to perish but to reach maturity with fully developed capacities, then free reign had to be given to it in its period of formation and growth. The medieval ruins, those mountain-top castles, those heaven-striving cathedrals, are the physical images of this spirit, as the Christian era, the Middle Ages, was the heroic age, the childish era which was to precede the mature era of mankind.

Christian life expressed itself now unmistakably; but out of the spirit which became powerful, the spirit of Christ himself began to vanish. This period created the immortal monuments, the living memorials of Christendom, which bear witness to all future generations of its presence and character. In David's time, during the prime of the Jewish nation, Zion was conquered and the Temple built. The motives for a similar deed – but here merely of spiritual nature – led to similar consequences. The Cross was preached; Jerusalem, the City of the Lord, was conquered; and all people cried out: 'This is the will of God.' For two centuries, innumerable masses of armed, warring people flowed from the Occident towards the Orient.

(28)

But at the same time, as spirituality had power in its hands, it became arrogant, and an abomination to God and man. The Christian Church had reached the zenith of its being: it slid into its decline as unimpeded as it had earlier moved towards its apex. In its prime, German minnesingers, French troubadours, and English minstrels sang the Psalms and the Song of Songs. Zealots for the waning spirit of Christ announced a bit later the decline of a corrupt era, the arrival of a new one. At the same time, reason and spirit began to be dominant and to replace fantasy, which was predominant in the first half of the period. In the teaching of Peter Waldus, who found many followers in this period, we discern the first indications of the new dawning light, which manifested itself later as Protestantism. And the fifth agony of the period began. The Geislers, these living Jeremiads, shook the Christian lands with their lamentations. But at the beginning of the fourteenth century, when Boniface the Eighth sat on the See of Peter, the anger of Philip of France became inflamed against the insolence of the Pope. And he sent his counsellor Nogaret to Italy to chastise the Pope, who died due to the agony of this humiliation. And the following Pope, Clement the Fifth, had to move his seat from Rome to Avignon, which was within Philip's territory, so that he became lord over city and Pope. Thus began the Papal Exile, which lasted like the Jewish one for seventy years.

Sixth Period: South America. From John Wycliffe to Martin Luther

He is a heretic who contradicts the holy teaching by word, writing or deed.   Joh. Huss[10]

(29)

After seventy years had expired, the Pope returned to Rome. A new epoch had now begun in Christian Europe. The glitter of the Church started diminishing; Europe turned into itself, became more circumspect. There arose numerous complaints against the corruption of the Church, and demands were made for reform at its head as well as limbs. At the same time, truth, science, and art achieved a constantly wider space in Christian Europe, whose peoples were becoming more devout and discerning than ever before. The ideas which fell on fertile ground took root and pushed vigorously into the daylight. And the old errors crumbled and turned into dust, once the dawn of a new sun illuminated them and the fresh morning air breathed upon them. But as the getting-out-of-itself [*Aussichhinaustreten*] or blossoming of Christianity had the opposite meaning than that of Judaism, so did its turning-into-itself [*Insichgehen*] or ripening. The revealed life of Judaism was an absolute; therefore, what lay at its foundation was spiritual, and it proceeded from it and returned to it. The revealed life of Christianity, on the other hand, was spiritual;

---

[10] *Historia et monumenta M. J. Hus et Hieronymi Pragensis* (Nuremberg, 1715), I, p. 130 (my translation).

therefore what lay at its foundation was absolute, and it proceeded from it and returned to it.

The collapse of the magical power of the clergy was accompanied by that of the material power of the worldly tyrants; arbitrary rule had to yield to the emerging dominion of the law. In contrast to the analogous period in the old world – between Ezra and the Maccabeans, when the High Priests became dominant and the great republics of Athens and Rome emerged – it was the secular monarchy which now held sway. At the beginning of this period John Wycliffe emerged and made the first comprehensive attempts at reformation. He viewed the Pope as the Anti-Christ (even if he did not dare say so in public) and saw the Holy Scripture, to which he exhorted his listeners to return, as the only source of divine life. He translated the Bible into his vernacular and praised the reading of the word of God. And the teaching of Wycliffe proliferated and found resonance especially in Bohemia, where the pious and learned Johannes Huss became his deserving disciple. At the same time there emerged Barthold Schwarz, the inventor of gunpowder, Johannes Gutenberg, the inventor of the art of book printing, and Christopher Columbus, the discoverer of America.

(30)

This is the way it looked among the people, out of which grew the great men like the produce of the young earth in spring; yet it was different among the clergy. It was not yet humiliated enough and refused to bow to the demands of the period, the will of God. In contrast to the growing corruption of the clergy, progress took place in the life of the people. But as the unfavourable external conditions were contrasted by unsustainable ones in the inner life; as the arts and sciences awoke from their long, nightlike slumber into a new, powerful life, and the gunpowder and the art of book printing were invented – then the old errors came into close contact with the new wishes and interests of the people. There arose an obstinate fight among the Christians of that period between those who strove for Reformation and their enemies, who continued to cling, out of a variety of motives, to the old errors.

A great affliction arose once again in Christendom, as the enemies of Christ came away with victory. The reformers, with Huss at their head, were mishandled, burnt; [but] the stake of Huss and Hieronymus [of Prague] sparked a terrible fire in the souls of the Bohemians and Moravians. This fire burned for a whole century and spread further and further. And as the enemies of Christ began to believe that they had triumphed, because Providence had not yet manifested its will through a public miracle, and the Papists presumed to re-establish their dominion anew, hoping to be able to resume infinitely their ignominious trade in God's grace – then a son was born to Hans Luther at the annual fair at Eisleben and was christened Martin.

Seventh Period: North America From Martin Luther to Benedict Spinoza

A mighty fortress is our God, A bulwark never failing.   Luther[11]

(31)

The Christian Maccabean appeared, and through his courage, his devout zeal and his powerful word, provided pure Christianity with victory. When Luther realized that a peaceful compromise was impossible, he formally broke away from the Pope and received support from high and low. Thus the Christian Church lost, however, its unity due to the obstinacy of its callous clergy and the exaggerated zeal of the Protestants. Just as the zealous Maccabeans, by desiring exactly the opposite, were turned by Providence into the vehicle towards the complete dissolution of the Jewish state, [so] the same befell the zealous Protestants. They established the principle of free enquiry in order to have a weapon against the enemies of Christ; but they themselves did not take this weapon seriously, since they did not seek pure truth for its own sake: rather than the dominion of the Holy Spirit, [they preferred] the letter of the Gospel. This is why, failing to recognize the spirit of true religion and getting involved in contradictions, they became intolerant. But in that period numerous great men appeared, and this epoch made enormous strides forward.

(32)

As the spirit of enquiry had now been liberated from its shackles by Protestantism, the views about Christianity multiplied and sects were formed. The Protestants were united only in fighting their common enemy, Catholicism; but lacking a unifying spirit, conflicts arose among

[11] This follows Frederick Hedge's translation of Luther's *Eine feste Burg ist unser Gott*.

them; and just as the Protestants bore enmity towards Catholics, the latter felt the same towards them. Both went too far in their blind zeal. Just as among the Jews in the analogous period Pharisees and Sadducees confronted each other, so the Jesuits emerged simultaneously with the Protestants out of the womb of the time. Here as there, ambitious schemes intervened in religious quarrels. Christian Europe was shaken to its foundations, but there were no Romans here to take power in this European society which was falling apart. Europe was both Judea and Rome; all meaningful revolutions, which were carried out in the old world by external forces (with the stronger beating the weaker), had to be fought out in the new world inside itself. Europe – since Columbus the ruler of the globe – had to rejuvenate itself within itself. A terrible Thirty Years War raged through the heart of the continent, and during this last agony of Christendom our Master was born to Jewish parents.[12]

> And when all things shall be subdued unto him, then shall the Son also himself be subject unto him that put all things under him, that God may be all in all.   I Corinthians 15:28

> At that day ye shall know that I am in my Father, and ye in me, and I in you.   John 14:20

End of the Middle Holy History

Note

(33)

With Christ there begins the middle period of the Spirit, which can be described as its endeavour to search for eternal truth. As we have already mentioned in the previous Note, the passive activity of the Spirit came to its conclusion with Christ, as fantasy had already taken on and off so many notions, that it did not need any further accretion from the outside in order to gain the idea of eternal life.

This eternal idea began, then, with Christ: the divine did not stick any more to any form; what it recognized, this was the eternal being. It already felt, though as yet only darkly, blurred by fantastical images, that Life is all-encompassing and eternal, that God is all in all. But while on one hand the eternal idea did appear, it seemed on the other hand that the temporal

---

[12] The reference is to Spinoza, as made clear on p. 37.

notions still stood there without being imbued and ruled by the Spirit, and through their very existence challenged the truth. As mentioned before, the knowledge of God consists in the abolition of such qualities in the particular as well as in the general. We saw in the previous period how the divine souls which appear later unite in their higher fantasy into a living whole the previous ones, which are divided and scattered among warring [entities]. But the fantasy images brought together through the unity which a divine soul imbued in them, were still nothing more than a higher fantasy image, not yet an eternal idea. Because God, or Life, could still not be comprehended in an all-encompassing way, only through images, albeit grand ones; but these were still finite, so long as fantasy had not yet achieved its apex. No spirit existed yet which declined to imagine God in a finite way, because this spirit was nothing else than the unity of all fantasy images, which were assumed not to have yet exhausted themselves.

The first spirit which acknowledged God as all-encompassing and eternal was Christ. He was the first eternal idea, emerging from the fully developed fantasy, out of whose images such qualities were revealed, which were truly all-encompassing and eternal.

(34)

But this knowledge of God was as little fully formed as the fantasy of the earlier period, because fantasy was not suddenly subjected to the eternal idea and fully permeated and dominated by it. The battle between unity and difference, the discord within the growing individual, which we have noticed in the previous main period, started now afresh, but in an inverted way.

In the previous period, the earlier unity or soul related in a passive way to the inflow of the images pressing themselves against it from the outside, because the unity, which a divine soul brought from time to time into the various fantasy images, was not an eternal unity, only a higher fantasy image. It is for this reason that it did not stand up against it in an active and hostile way. Now, by contrast, the later unity stood up in an active and hostile way against all earlier notions of fantasy; the eternal idea, the Spirit, strove to pervade the different forms of life which existed previously. And just as such a striving dominated the internal life of the period, so it revealed itself externally as well. The Christians did not try to enrich themselves externally, to partake of external power. All that mattered to them was to animate all the nations of the earth, who still lived in wickedness, with their idea. But this did not happen suddenly, neither externally nor internally. Because every being tries to remain in its own proper existence, and people experienced as tough a resistance when they tried to dislodge the old fallacies as Nature [had experienced] in the earlier period, when it tried to enrich people's fantasy with images, which did not agree with their old ones.

(35)

During this whole period, the obstinate battle, which humanity had to fight out within itself, raged in manifold shades. It was the battle between fantasy and reason, during which both, as yet not overpowered, tried to persevere. While the idea of uniting all fantasy images tried incessantly to prevail, the fantastical imagination, which fought equally for its existence, did not give up; the one was tarnished by the other, the latter permeated by the former.

Just as earlier the new notions pressing from the outside on [the existing ones] heaped passively error upon error, so now truth confronted actively the error of the idea of notion, light confronted darkness, the higher human [confronted] the lower. Reason fought fantasy until it could reconcile itself with it and achieve a glorious peace. We say peace because in the highest consciousness, all fantasy images or notions exist– from the lowest sense perceptions up to the highest opinions – and live next to the eternal Idea, just as the lower forms of consciousness are ruled and guided by the higher ones. The fully formed Idea recognizes every form of consciousness; only it does not lose sight of what is lacking in the lower form. Fully formed reason, for example, recognizes the belief in God, freedom, and immortality; yet it repudiates the false notions of fantasy that lead men astray towards numerous deceptions by which these eternal verities, of which all living beings are aware whether darkly or clearly, are reflected in more or less sensual, temporal, or spatial forms. Likewise, reason does not deny the lowest sense perceptions; but by holding them to be what they truly are, i.e. one-sided, superficial forms of consciousness, they are subjected to a higher judgment, submitted to its supervision and ruled and guided by it.

(36)

But until in this way all life, or every form of consciousness, can live side by side peacefully, conflict and strife rule living and constantly moving nature, until fully developed humanity comes into its own. In the present period we see this contrast within humanity persist; we discern a battle between man and man. This battle is the herald of eternal peace; because when the contrast reaches its apex, it moves towards its reconciliation. This contrast, based on temporal life, i.e. beginning in lower consciousness and then moving to the higher one, is, as mentioned, constantly overcome [*aufgehoben*] through the unity of the Spirit; but on the other hand [it] is being constantly renewed though the dissolution of fantasy, whose rule has not yet been concluded and which has not yet been subordinated. One notices in this period a troublesome striving of the Spirit, sunk into itself and alien to life, which Börne has called 'the curse of what is born in sorrow'.[13] In reality this is a dangerous crisis, which decides on life and death so long as it can act undisturbed – and then it brings forth to the world a ripe fruit; or, if disturbed by untimely obstructions, exaggerations, or hindrances, it gives birth to a crippled, often dead fruit. In the history of mankind this period found its time and place so as to act undisturbed.

(37)

In the Christian epoch the contrast between truth and falsehood held out until it exhausted itself in all parts, until its trace was dissolved in the progress of time. The Spirit sank into the depth of its own soul, and searched and meditated so long until it laid the foundation for truth. We shall presently see the divine fruit, which emerged from this intense middle period. Incidentally, the similarity which we noticed regarding the course of history between this period and the preceding one, justifies the verdict that this course, even if we do not totally comprehend its law, is not accidental but necessary, and we shall have to discover it again in the next period. We shall see how proceeding in history, this conclusion is being confirmed by experience.

---

[13] Ludwig Börne, 'Fragmente und Aphorismen', in *Gesammelte Schriften* (Hamburg, 1829), VI, p. 141. The literary allusion is to God's curse on Eve (Genesis 3:16): 'in sorrow thou shalt bring forth children'.

CHAPTER THREE

The Third Main Period of the Holy History – or the History of Revelation of God, the Holy Spirit

Even as light displays both itself and darkness, so is truth a standard both of itself and of falsity.   ETHICS II, 43 NOTE[1]

The mind's highest good is the knowledge of God, and the mind's highest virtue is to know God.   ibid., IV, 28[2]

First Period: North America From Benedict Spinoza to the French Revolution

Europe is dying.
Joh. Müller[3]

(38)

As our Master appeared, Christ has triumphed. And once again, a period has come to the end of its cycle. The history of revelation of God the Son – or the knowledge of God in the feelings of the soul – which has until now dominated the earth, has been fulfilled and closed. With our immortal Teacher, the foundations of the new age have been laid; with him began the history of revelation of God [as] the Holy Spirit, or the purest knowledge of God. When Spinoza was fully formed [*ausgebildet*],

---

[1] *The Chief Works of Benedict de Spinoza*, trans. R. H. M. Elwes (new editon; New York, 1951), II, p. 115. This quote from Spinoza, as well as all subsequent ones, is quoted by Hess from a German translation of *The Ethics*, and not in the original Latin.

[2] Ibid., p. 205.

[3] Despite the reference to Müller's book already mentioned by Hess, such a quote could not be found in his works. Hess might be referring to a general impression he got from the author's work.

37

he united once again, like his ancestors Adam and Christ, the conflicts of his age in his divine soul into a living whole. And once again, he saw more than his predecessors and deeper than his contemporaries; for he recognized God who is Life. For God revealed himself to him not in the feelings of the soul, but in the bright light of reason. He who was full of his spirit, was lifted beyond the old quarrels of opinion about the letter of the Gospel, because he comprehended God purely spiritually and honoured him through truth.

The first enlightened persons were pure people, for whom what mattered was truth and human welfare. But as the Enlightenment spread around, there arose many degenerate deviations in various directions. Because once more the old world had sunk, and as the new learning spread within it, monstrous off-springs appeared in corrupted souls. The history of this era is still fresh in the memories of our brethren. Once divided Christianity ceased to be the soul of Europe, an ambitious, unholy politics appeared in its stead, because Christianity had lost unity, power, and life, but no new spirit had yet been breathed into the dying Europe. Separate parties professed different Christian denominations, and therefore there was no one religion for the whole [of Europe]. It was a transition from one main period to another, and the germ of the new period was sown in the moment the old one began to die. But this germ was not yet visible, and it grew internally without having much influence on the great affairs of the world.

The Westphalian accords gave the continent a sort of a peace, but only an external one, not an internal peace of the soul. People tolerated each other not out of conviction, but because they lacked the power to vanquish each other. This was not genuine tolerance, which acknowledges the other's singular life and allows it to live peacefully next to one's own. The authority of a divine soul was replaced by a precarious, seesaw-like system of balance of power. And just as in ageing Rome, after it had lost its virtue, Emperors and Praetorians held sway over debased citizens, slaves, and puppets, so the same occurred in the ageing Europe: 'The priests have lost their power; soldiers ruled a world moved only slightly by ideas. There was no trace any more of a will, of an independent life among the people. All movement emanated from the courts, whose levers are intrigues, money and arms' (v. Rotteck).[4]

---

[4] C. von Rotteck, *Allgemeine Geschichte vom Anfang der historischen Erkenntniss bis auf unsere Zeiten* (Freiburg i. B., 1830), VIII, p. 36.

(39)

But a spirit grew in the innermost entrails of the period, ready to create new forms once the old ones had collapsed. This was the Holy Spirit of truth, justice, and love. And in the last half of this period it announced its future life through joyful leaps and all kinds of movements in the womb of the mother; the symptoms of its life became undeniable. At the time, a true quest for Enlightenment reigned supreme; everyone who felt the electrical spark of the new era could not imagine being less than zealous in carrying it further. And the intangible living spark spread despite all corruption and enslavement, because God had awakened great fighters for the new age, and led the hearts of the high and mighty [towards it]. Holy science grew among the people and on the thrones; it was driven by a zeal unknown until now, reaching an unheard-of range.

At the same time the Jesuits – these ghosts of the old times, who shied away from the light – were abandoned by their protectors and banished by them. Just as it was once the teaching of Christ, truth was now wonderfully defended and propagated in the midst of all sinfulness and slavery. Now and then, the dying period raised its head once again in last convulsions. The Pope made a last journey, addressed a final request of grace to [the Habsburg] Emperor Joseph – and had to turn back and return home without having his wishes fulfilled. Already the new age was swinging its knife and cutting away the diseased parts of the old [age], in order to avoid a gangrenous infection. It achieved its first victory across the ocean, where at the beginning of this period free communities organized themselves, just as during the Roman Empire the first Christian communities [had appeared]. It looked as if they first grew overseas out of caution, to cover their back should they be defeated on this side [of the ocean]; but in reality, they were defiant, and grew naturally where there were fewest impediments.

[But] when culture spread from the southwest to the northeast, it came back by the paved route. On this side, a terrible revolution was spreading, similar in its consequences to those which occurred in the wake of Adam and Christ. Through the history of revelation of God the Holy Spirit one can perceive once more the voice of the Lord announcing the Day of Judgment: 'לא ידון רוחי'.[5] And when the time allocated to the old world ran out, the hostile forces appeared against each other.

---

[5] 'My spirit shall not always strive with man' (Genesis 6:3; see above, note 11). This appears in the original Hebrew in Hess' text.

Second Period: Europe. The Revolution

Do you hear the little bell ringing? Kneel down. They are bringing
the sacraments to a dying God.   Heinrich Heine[6]

(40)

It was neither a deluge of water, as happened after Adam, nor a deluge
of nations, as happened after Christ, but a deluge of ideas which arose
ominously out of the womb of the era: and it destroyed everything which
stood in its way. Let us consider ourselves as a child of the great Revolution
which originated in France and has rejuvenated the continent! Few doubt
that it has given birth to a new era; yet who but we constitute this new era?
Some would hold that the child entered the world stillborn, since it has
not yet given a reasonable sign of life. Yet those who maintain this forget
that at birth the higher individual does not immediately bring with itself
its fully formed spirit, unlike an animal with its instincts. The first signs
of life of the noblest creature known to us are shouts and naughtiness; it is
indeed through shouts and naughtiness that the new era has sufficiently
announced itself. Initially, these signs of life were the only ones possible –
the natural; and while philistines bemoan the destructive anger and dis-
array brought by the child into the home, we discern in its expressions
only its energy and liveliness, and our heart jumps with joy when we contemplate the future of this living being. Weak souls, who always swim on
the surface because they lack breath for deep diving, tearfully lament the
horrors of the great French Revolution. But we recognize God's majesty in
the threatening thunderstorm just as in a friendly sunshine, in the bloody
battlefield as in the peaceful fruit-bearing field. Pedants recoil from the
man of the Movement, not realizing that in a whole people powerful life
must unmistakably produce, sooner or later, something valuable; and that
a vain idolatry of what is dying prevents any genuine renewal. These words
of Raumer[7] about the world's rejuvenation after Christ can be applied in
their fullest meaning also to the world's rejuvenation after Spinoza.

---

[6] Heinrich Heine, *History of Religion and Philosophy in Germany*, trans. Helen M. Mustard,
in *Selected Works* (New York, 1973), p. 265. This work of Heine has been a major source for
Hess' reading of modern history, including the emphasis on Spinoza as the harbinger of the
modern age and his unique integration of the Judaic tradition into the modern philosophical
discourse.

[7] Raumer, *Geschichte.*, I, p. 7.

(41)

With the French Revolution – about which Mirabeau had prophesied that it would encircle the world in its progress – the third and last emergence of humanity out of its cocoon has begun; however, this process is not yet over. We can already discern the wings of the young butterfly, while others, exhausted by the frightening metamorphosis, wish to get back into the form of a caterpillar – just as the Israelites in the desert yearned for the flesh pots of Egypt, despite the slavery awaiting them there.

About our own era there prevail the greatest misconceptions and the most differing opinions: because historical scenes – like natural scenes or fresco paintings and all great objects – can be adequately reviewed only from a certain distance. One usually contemplates the period in which one lives as looking at infusoria through a microscope; but, like a giant, the period has to be viewed from a proper distance.

(42)

As Napoleon's star began to wane in the East, just like that of Attila, the old barbarian oppressor of the peoples had begun to wane in the West, and later – after a short renewed flickering – was finally extinguished; after Europe was liberated from that mighty ruler who was destined to rejuvenate the continent, but not to nurse the young world, many believed that the revolution had come to its end. And there was much truth in this opinion; but there were also people who maintained that the child, born in much pain, had been garrotted, and one should begin to restore the old order once again. The Vienna Congress, much addicted to this delusion, was able to restore to the divided Europe of the nineteenth century as little of its internal peace as the Westphalian [peace] was able to bestow it on seventeenth-century Europe. Many have not yet grasped this. Next to malicious egoists there also existed in all times shortsighted fools, who – because they lacked an insight into the future – looked for salvation in a past that could not be resurrected. Among such people, whose weak spirit clung hard to idols without their heart being corrupted, and who had once heard that the past is the root of the future and should not therefore be written off – but who do not know the meaning of this eternal truth – among these people, we say, there exist failed windbags who naively extol science as a counterweight to that death which they do not comprehend. Those idiots, they do not imagine that it is holy science[8] alone which created and nourished our era and will lift it also up to that throne to which it has been destined by Eternity. The malicious ones are more consistent than those fools; they strive to produce an artificial solar eclipse and close the windows in bright daylight, in order to persuade the world that night has fallen; with this they deceive only children.

But let us return to history.

(43)

After the battle of Belle Alliance there began a so-called Restoration not only in France, the birthplace of the Revolution, but also in the rest of Europe. This, however, was not in the spirit of the time [*Geist der Zeit*]; therefore it lacked a goal. The battle in the inner souls continued; the spirit of the time glimmered quietly, like a muffled but not extinguished fire, for fifteen years; it continued to expand, occasionally also broke out. But the building masters continued building recklessly on the sites whose foundations had been eroded long ago by the fires of the times. And lo and behold! When they reached the roof and wished to set the crown on their edifice, the whole building collapsed! Because fire broke out of the entrails of the earth and suddenly swallowed all the pestilential prison odours – just as in the time of the creation, when God said: 'Let there be light.'[9]

(44)

And the stronger child of the time did not make as much noise as at its first appearance, because it had become calmer in the consciousness of its life. Now it became more reasonable and appeared to smile at the old auntie who again pushed herself forward and tried to wrap it once again in diapers, under the pretext that it should not suffer any harm. Six years have passed since the old snake had tried cunningly to embrace

---

[8] The term used by Hess is *Wissenschaft*, which in the German philosophical tradition as well in everyday speech encompasses not only the natural science, but the totally of human knowledge (*epistēmē*). Thus Hegel's main philosophical compendium was entitled *Die Enzyklopädie der philosophischen Wissenschaften*, and what is called in English 'Humanities' is termed in German '*Geisteswissenschaften*': to translate this as 'Spiritual *Sciences*' would, of course, be absurd.

[9] Genesis 1:3.

and entangle the child of man, in order to strangle it when opportunity came.[10] But its time is up.

> And I saw a new heaven and a new earth: for the first heaven and the first earth were passed away; and there was no more sea.
>
> (Revelation 21:1)

Note

(45)

We have the third kind of consciousness before us, the fruit of a stressful era, which can be designated as the spiritually purest form of the knowledge of God. The striving of the Spirit is satisfied in this way, and this satisfaction is the highest possible. It is true that the Spirit, in its pursuit of truth, continues in its striving, since God is inexhaustible. But both the active striving of the Spirit, as well as the passive activity of the soul, are being dominated and guided by mankind which now unites in itself both kinds of spiritual activities, the masculine and the feminine. Once the human creature has regained its unity and recognized God in his depth as well as in his width, it has been relieved of the tiresome search for its life's aim. Man now knows how to arrange feeling and acting in line with a perceived law and proceeds in the path of eternal life in God with clear consciousness and a firm, quiet, and manly stride. He is enriched from the outside through the passive activity of his soul while independently bringing unity into diversity internally.

No longer does one notice that striving, directed unto himself and inimical to external life, which persisted in the human spirit during the previous period. Because the split between the lower and the higher nature of man, between fantasy and reason, has been forever overcome. Mankind has regained its lost child-like simplicity; it has regained it so as never to lose it again. The third kind of consciousness is an eternally serene fountain of pure love of God, a passion for life and bliss. He who possesses it, his bliss and serenity are unassailable, because nothing appears inimical to him, so that the unity of his consciousness remains permanently saved. Inside the individual, who possesses the third kind of knowledge of God, no form of strife or repugnance can arise; hence the source of vice and evil is choked, and only freedom and joy dwell in him.

---

[10] This is an obvious but veiled reference to the 1830 Revolution in France.

In order to demonstrate this, we need nothing less than a detailed explication of the teaching of salvation bequeathed to us by the Master. But in the present volume, which has its own aim, this cannot be achieved.

(46)

So noiseless was the beginning of the revelation history of God the Holy Spirit that even now many, who seek truth only for their own sake, have not yet grasped the significance of the man in whose fully developed teaching lies its true life. This singularity in the appearance of the realm of truth, this spiritual manifestation, which is so totally lacking in every external and material sign and miracle, is not without minor advantages for truth itself. On the one hand, it will shield us from superstitious believers; on the other, it will defend our latter brethren – as it did our earlier ones – from the old delusion that God's revelations to mankind are not necessary phenomena, subject to the laws of the times like all others in nature, but rather teachings provided by God in a way which is supernatural and contrary to reason; and – consequently – that what is needed from this point of view is a merely arbitrary, formal confession, not a living recognition, an essential religion. This [history of revelation] will prove that it is not those, through whom the Spirit reveals itself, who can be called the real creators of their epoch (because God alone is the living source and creator of all times), but rather that they themselves become such through the eternal law of the times, which – in its turn – needs them.

(47)

With Spinoza there began no other period than that for which Christ had yearned, for which he and his first disciples and all of Christendom have hoped and prophesied. The period of the Holy Spirit has arrived, the Kingdom of God, the New Jerusalem which has been the consolation of every Christian. But while this divine kingdom has not been recognized by many and is being viewed by them with hostility, when in the future it still will be hated and persecuted by men, then this should not lead us – who are convinced of its existence – astray. For we have learned from Adam that during a new revelation there always are also those who are stuck in the old one and cling to it with tooth and nail – and their very existence becomes proof of the progress of the divine revelation in the world of men.

How can a true Christian – one who is convinced of the world-historical significance of Christ – find offence in the Kingdom of God because many still lag behind and distance themselves from him, since he [should] see that such a lagging behind is grounded in nature? After all, only a handful of Jews joined in the mission of Christ, while the great majority lagged behind. And the Jews themselves were the descendants of the third man through whom God revealed himself to mankind. The great majority of the noble people lagged behind, and did not partake in the Old Law – to which Moses responded with the following words: 'The Lord did not set his love upon you, nor choose you, because ye were more in number than any people; for ye were the fewest of all people' (Deuteronomy 7:7). Others point to the antiquity of the religion which they recognize and are thus taken aback when having to march with the spirit of the age. But regarding this [new] epoch, which many regard with distaste, [it is obvious] that no man, if he could have been present at his own creation and had been asked, would have said: 'I would rather be an animal and not a human being, because the animal kingdom came first.' And no animal – had it possessed rational speech and been able to speak – would have said: 'I would rather remain in the kingdom of plants, because it is older.'

But just as the realm of man is different from that of the animals, and that of the animals is different from that of the plants in spatial terms, so in spiritual terms the kingdom of reason is distinct from the Christian and the latter from the Jewish one. But just as the realm of animals emerged according to nature out of that of the plants, and the realm of men out of that of animals, so out of the Jewish realm there arose the Christian, and out of the latter there arose the realm of truth.

(48)

Just as Christ did not wish to overturn through his teaching the Old Law, in so far as it was divine, but only to widen it, so Spinoza repudiated neither the Christian nor the Jewish religion, in so far as they were divine. Rather, besides presenting his own teachings, he expressed himself quite clearly about the old ones. He wrote a separate treatise in which, as he says himself, he attempted to show that theology and philosophy – faith and knowledge – can indeed live peacefully alongside each other.[11] Anyone who has understood the Master's teaching correctly can have no doubt about this. Just as fantasy and feeling can – as we have already shown in the previous Note – live peacefully next to reason, unhurt in their rights granted to them by Nature – so can Jews and Christians live side by side, so long as they are of divine nature and not split in themselves or sinful. Only the enemies of truth are our enemies; consequently, all those who are not yet as advanced as we are in the knowledge of God are not our enemies. Spinoza teaches this in the following words: 'All ideas, in so far as they are referred to God, are true . . . There is nothing positive in ideas, which causes them to be called false . . . No positive quality possessed by a false idea is removed by the presence of what is true, in virtue of its being true' (*Ethics* II, 32, 33; IV, 1).[12] It is also self-evident that truth does not invalidate what is true or positive in a fallacy: only that which is false is being rejected though the recognition of truth, so that the fallacy is being cleansed, not destroyed.

(49)

Faith is the foundation of knowledge just as fantasy is the foundation of reason. The first relates to the latter as soul to spirit. That people do not make the right distinctions, but go too far either in merely one or in many directions and confuse everything – this was and remains the original sin out of which arise wickedness, blindness, eternal intolerance.

We should not proceed here without drawing attention to the mis-leading paths of recent philosophies which went so far, on the one hand, as to place God himself in the centre of the world, to think of him, this absolute infinite Life, as the Soul of the World – or, on the other hand, there surfaced the opposite extreme that God, as the World Spirit, has a history! We clearly recognize here the eternal law of all times, that the original One is being split in order to be united later in a higher life.

It is obvious that the two philosophers who are mentioned here have divided among themselves the teaching of the Master. The time has, how-ever, come to point out that both, because they wished to blend together, each in a contrary way, two distinct concepts, had in reality split apart

---

[11] The reference is to Spinoza's *Tractatus Theologico-Politicus*.
[12] *The Chief Works of Benedict de Spinoza*, II, pp. 108, 191.

the true One, i.e. God. We do not wish in any way to deny the high value of both of these philosophies: rather, we recognize each of them in its sphere. Schelling's contribution to the natural sciences is as undisputed as that of Hegel in the study and investigation of history. Only in so far as each of these philosophies asserts that it is absolute knowledge, a teaching of salvation, do we deny their claim. Since salvation resides in the absolute, all-encompassing knowledge of God, one cannot seek it either in the philosophy of nature or in the philosophy of the spirit.

God, or Life, can not be comprehended exclusively in nature, or thought of as spirit: because under 'Spirit' we understand what is relatively conscious, individual, under 'Nature' that which is relatively without consciousness, universal. Man, as the spirit of the earth, is merely one form of God; he is the relatively individual. Animals, plants, stones, ultimately earth itself as the foundation of their organization, are equally merely kinds of Life; they are the relatively universal. Here the soul, unity, is dominant and the spirit, or consciousness, stands back; while in the former, in contrast, spirit dominates, while the soul – as experience has unfortunately confirmed too often in the life of mankind – recedes into the background.

There can be no true life either without consciousness, or without soul. Man represents the relatively advanced form – history, or time; the lower forms of consciousness represent the relatively enduring – nature, or space. Life, however, does not reside exclusively in the one or the other, either in repose, or in movement – but in both.

In order to go back to what we have already said: salvation should not be sought exclusively either in belief or in knowledge, either in Schelling's blissful devotion of the soul, or in Hegel's spiritual religion of the concept; either in feeling, or in reason, either in repose, or in movement, either in the past, or in the future: rather it is both – not flowing into each other or mixed together, but peacefully existing one beside the other – that constitute true Life in such a way that the lower consciousness, faith, is subordinated to higher knowledge, dominated and guided by it. Obviously the lower forms of consciousness cannot acknowledge the higher ones, since they know them not; the higher, on the other hand, who know the lower, because they have permeated them – as all forms of life, as they come one after the other in the individual, also continue to exist side by side – have to acknowledge them if they do not want to split Life wretchedly or to melt it into a grayish mass.

(50)

As mentioned, Spinoza does put in doubt the sanctity of the Scriptures and says explicitly that prophecy is an endowment of fantasy, but not of reason. It follows from this, as well as from other statements, that he acknowledges the divinity of fantasy, that he admits the possibility that fantasy can be as holy as reason – an important admission which is however being overlooked by one of his admirers (Schleiermacher)[13] – which would indeed cause a serious deficiency in his teaching of salvation. We admit that in so far as reason predominates in our Master, fantasy is relegated to the background: he acknowledges this himself. Because he says (in Chapter II of *Tractatus Theologico-Politicus*[14]) that those who are endowed with a large imagination are less capable of comprehending things in a pure fashion, while those who possess more reason and cultivate it suitably are capable of a more modest imagination. Moreover, he maintains explicitly (ibid., Chapter I[15]) that he does not know according to which laws of nature revelation takes place. Yet at the same time he clearly recognizes that there exists a holy fantasy – and with this he closes his theological treatises by hailing the use and necessity of revelation (i.e. fantasy and feeling) for the salvation of mankind so long as it is not ripe for pure rational knowledge. Regarding divinity or the blissful unity of consciousness, the man of fantasy does not lack anything as compared to the man of reason. As we have remarked in the opening of this Note, truth is holy, imparts to its friends an undisturbed bliss, an unclouded, moral consciousness, because there exists nothing which can be in unfriendly contrast or contradiction to it. But we have shown (§§ 15, 16, 48) that the unity of consciousness can be brought about also through fantasy; hence in the sphere of ethics, the man of fantasy is not different from the man of reason.

Just as there exists divine reason, divine fantasy can also exist, and just as there can exist a godless fantasy, so there can also exist godless reason. Fantasy is distinguished from reason only in that the latter is conscious of God or truth under the aegis of eternity, affirmation, and consequence, and of godlessness or lie under the aegis of destruction, denial, and inconsequence; while [fantasy] becomes conscious of God

[13] The reference is to Friedrich Daniel Schleiermacher's *Grundlinien einer Kritik der bisherigen Sittenlehre*.
[14] *The Chief Works of Benedict de Spinoza*, I, 'A Theologico-Political Treatise', pp. 27–42.
[15] Ibid., pp. 13–26.

under the sign of beauty and harmony, and of godlessness through ugliness and disharmony.

Feeling too has its images for divinity and godlessness, namely Heaven and Hell, sublimity and baseness, and so on. All these different forms do not change essentially anything. Thus the Holy Spirit appeared to the Christians in the form of a dove, namely as love and tenderness, though it has already revealed itself in many other forms.

Had it been our aim to discuss here the subjects of ethics, then we would have to go into much more detail. But as already said, this is not our aim: we would, however, like to make in passing the important comment that our enemy is not what is old – but all those who are wicked and impure; and that among those who are new, and who call themselves our brethren, there are as many enemies of truth as among the old. Providence will, however, bring about the Kingdom of God, despite internal and external enemies.

(51)

Equally, following the Master's own teaching, we have to remark that we should acknowledge the divine revelation only in so far as it promotes our salvation – the knowledge of God – and not in that it comprises other matters, which do not relate to our individual-moral and social-human life transformation; similarly, those people whom we describe in the holy history as 'men of the epoch' have to be seen as such only in a practical sense. We say this not in order to assuage the conscience of those who have already committed themselves to the teaching of the Master, since these, when they truly recognize the teaching, must already know this. We say this only to those who are still unfamiliar with this new divine teaching and could therefore imagine it would be impossible to profess a positive teaching or a revealed religion without limiting – as it had been until now – one's own free judgment, since truth has not yet been taught or believed in all its purity.

It is only in the Holy Spirit, which holds sway in the divine revelation, and not in the dead word, that we have to believe and to be confirmed in it. If we do not follow this view and would stick to the letter, we would contradict ourselves immediately – like the Christians who stick to the letter and imagine that truth is comprised only in a certain limited and sealed collection of books. In this they put the spirit in chains and maintain that there is no living progress in the revelation of God to mankind – something which the Jews equally believe and justifiably use as a weapon against the Christians, though it speaks also against them.

Neither the Jews, even less so the Christians, and least of all we, can maintain this without an inner contradiction. Only those who close [their] eyes and ears, or who are blind and deaf by nature, could deny that both before and after them the Holy Spirit of God holds sway in history. Only essence alone – God – is an unchanging One, but his revelations vary, change, move forward in time.

(52)

All that has been said can be summed up in a few words: God, or life, appears in pure fantasy just as it appears in pure reason: [it appears] as unity, yet is still figurative, imprisoned in temporal attributes. In pure consciousness the eternal idea of God struggles with the limited notion of the same in such a way that pure consciousness expresses a constant prayer, an uninterrupted yearning, a never-silenced yearning and hope that this discord will be overcome. In pure reason God is finally perceived once again as unity, just as in pure fantasy – but as eternal truth, without temporal, transient attributes.

(53)

It would be highly deceptive, and contrary to the essence of the Holy Spirit, to believe that with the third revelation a new religion has begun, a teaching of God which is contrary to the previous ones: there exists only one eternal religion, and it is this ancient religion which is being revealed here in the illuminated garment of the spirit. In this we think we have encountered a fallacy which has caused much strife in the world – the father of intolerance and fanaticism – and therefore we [try to] explain the essence of the Holy Spirit in this Note. The Master himself warned us of this dangerous delusion in having expressed the wish to promote the knowledge of God and not to stick any more to words. We would also have kept totally quiet about the significance of the man who, without saying so explicitly, constitutes the invisible soul of our epoch, if we did not feel that it is our vocation to contribute to the understanding of history.

As we have already remarked, the flowing into each other and blending together of the various periods of history, as well as of different forms of nature, is as detrimental to understanding as the splitting apart of the eternal, one essence. When we want to blur the different characteristics, the reason is that we confuse form with essence, and death is then brought in also from the other end just as from the side of those who would like to split everything. The latter [bring death] through dispersion and dissolution, and the false unifiers through binding and chaining. By the way, those who would like to call the Master's teaching of salvation by another name are free to call it, according to their wish, the 'kernel' or the 'soul' of the revelation history of 'God the Holy Spirit'. We are totally in agreement with them if they only comprehend the divine content of the teaching: we would not like to fight over words. Naturally we find no reason for preferring God's revelation through fantasy or feeling to that through reason and call it 'revelation' or 'the knowledge of God'. We also think it preferable for understanding to maintain the traditional, popular expressions, rather than adopt a new scholarly language.

(54)

Because man, as he actually lives and strives, being subject to one-sidedness and fallacy, would have been forsaken by inner peace and would lose his bliss and descend into desperation, if in times of need a supporting hand were not offered to him, a beacon, towards which his spiritual glance could strive to pull him out of the surrounding darkness; therefore weak man recognizes and acknowledges in his despair this holy bond by coming closer to God and thus being strengthened. True religion – the knowledge of the positively revealed spirit of God, who marches through history in the holy tradition and Scripture, and through nature through the holy deed – this religion is the eternal support of weak man. Every being has the law of God engraved in its soul; yet the historically progressing spirit of man has to have a guide so that the law of the Eternal would be revealed to him in the apparent lawlessness of the times, as would harmony in the midst of chaos, unity in diversity. The Holy Spirit is this guide – natural religion is not enough for man.

An Interlude (instead of an Introduction) to a correct judgment of these pages

(1)

With the passing of time the knowledge of God has become confused. The more subtle our wisdom, the more multifaceted has our stupidity become. Had God's grace not endured eternally, what would have become of us? . . . Men have once again reached the point where they are lost without a compass in a sea of errors, finding themselves in the middle of a Noahite deluge of ideas. Where is the ark, where is deliverance? In a time in which humility is paraded for show, because at heart it nourishes pride, it would sound ridiculous if somebody came forth and announced: here is the ark, here is deliverance! And yet all those who have become conscious of their calling have said exactly that, without appearing to lose their divine standing because of this. This however came about because they have not sworn allegiance to their ephemeral 'I', this idol of a million forms, and have reckoned as an achievement what we have to acknowledge solely as the grace of the eternal, immeasurable God: because they were as far from the idol-worship of pride as are those meek ones who aid it with courtly words. Religion, the knowledge of God, the highest good of man, was lost, and the finder should be ashamed to call out in joy: here it is again!? Truly, it is against this humility that his conscience rebels. Let the arrogant smile at him pityingly, the jealous foam at the mouth, the obscurantists and fanatics persecute him: he, however, announces his findings loudly and uncompromisingly, because this is how the voice of the Lord commands him.

Therefore we do not hesitate to declare openly that, in so far as the idea described in these pages was clearly announced to us, we see ourselves as

a humble instrument of eternal Providence, which has in all times lov-
ingly preferred to be served by people who have lived in darkness and
baseness – so that man will truly feel and finally recognize his own impo-
tence and the omnipotence of divine grace dwelling in him!

(2)

The history of mankind is undoubtedly that field of knowledge which
sheds the greatest light on men in their social and spiritual relationship.
But the way history has been perceived until now – despite the praiseworthy attempts of [our] time to discern a plan in world history – it has still
not become a systematic science, but only an amassing of experiences, out
of which a few truths could be deduced, but which did not allow us, by
and large, to reach any conclusions. In these pages the attempt is being
made to bring order into chaos, to attempt for the first time to conceive
world history in its totality and [discover] its laws. It is natural that this
first attempt is as incomplete as the language of a child who has only
just begun to learn to speak. But nobody would be so cruel as to forbid
the child from trying to speak because its language is not yet perfect. We
are far from presuming to erect an edifice of learning, which can appear
perfect only when mankind itself is fully developed. But this should not
hinder us from building as far as our power goes.

(3)

Well-ordered history will shed light on that religion, to which the best
part of mankind vows allegiance, just as we owe to that religion alone the
enlightenment with which we have been graced by Providence. Religion
and history have an inner relationship to each other; the one elucidates
the other. A being which is still without spirit and consciousness has no
religion and no history, because it is not in a position to recognize God.
Only man made spiritual hangs by an invisible chain – called tradition –
which stretches from the first man, borne by Mother Earth, up to the last
one, whom she will again welcome to her bosom.

(4)

Through the wide chain of a messy tradition there leads a delicate thread,
which can show us the way through the labyrinth if we take the trouble

to hold on to it and not to cut it off with a crude hand. It is this delicate thread which we referred to as the holy history of mankind, and to whose unpretentious representation these pages are dedicated. We have brought it to the light of day – and it must be left to the higher situated spirits of the future to follow its trail further, to fathom its significance more deeply.

(5)

Regarding our interpretation of the tradition of Adam, we have though to mention explicitly that we would not like to place the beginning of the existence of human beings in that epoch with which this tradition starts: we are taught by an unprejudiced and unconstrained exegesis of the holy tradition that long before [Adam] the earth has been populated by human creatures of a lower sort. As far as we can gather according to our conviction from the text of Genesis and from the analogy offered to us by the whole holy history of mankind, one should understand under the נְפִילִים' in Genesis a pre-worldly (pre-Adamite) human race, whose day of judgment appeared after Adam with the flood of water, just as that of the ancient Jews and the pagans appeared with the flood of peoples after Christ, and that of the old Christians with the flood of ideas after Spinoza. This fable (see Part I, §2) appears as an explanation of the previous story of depravity, and its last words allude to the many scattered stories telling of heroes and gods. We are not being told here clearly who the 'Nephilim' were, nor when and whence they have appeared. Since we are told here that the period referred to occurred 'in those days' (ibid. [Genesis 6:4]), that is, in the period between Adam and the deluge, then the 'Nephilim' must have lived on earth next to the 'Adamites' and are supposed to have fallen, as previously believed, from heaven: either one totally relegates this tradition to the great realm of myth, as not having any historical foundation (this is obviously the easiest manner to seal oneself off from stories which do not immediately fit into our understanding: here, however, this seems even more dubious, as this tradition, in its account and explication, leads towards a higher and clearer consciousness). [Alternatively] one may assume that next to the noble human beings there existed other human creatures. Therefore we believe that with Adam there began a new period in the history of the earth, namely

---

' 'Nephilim' (Genesis 6:4): usually translated as 'giants', though the Hebrew etymology points to 'the fallen ones'; hence the tradition, both Judaic and Christian, about 'fallen angels'.

the period of the Holy Spirit of the history of noble humanity. It should be mentioned that our view is being confirmed geologically when one understands the word נפילים as meaning 'giants'.

In order to avoid misunderstandings, we have further to stress that when we speak in these pages of certain individuals or peoples as chosen, we do not maintain by this that they were the only godly ones in their epoch. Neither do we believe that they were the only ones, or that they were exclusively the godliest; rather that of all those who appeared on earth according to the laws of nature they were the most superior in the practical sense. So we do not maintain, for example, that at first only one pair emerged of the noble human species: but we maintain that if many did emerge, only one among them was superior in the mentioned meaning. According to our view, it is the *noblest* pair that is to be understood as the *first*, of which the holy tradition reports. The same applies, it appears self-evident, to the rest of the chosen men and people, whom we see emerging in the history of mankind out of the womb of time.

At the conclusion of the First Part we would only like to remark that the pages presented here can be understood only with difficulty if viewed separately, in as much as the whole is one idea, and the last word must serve to elucidate the earlier one.

(6)

After we have allowed the past to unfold before us, we continue to build on this firm foundation. While doing this, we have to defend ourselves from a false suspicion under which one falls easily in our time – namely, that we intend to bring about or stir up revolutions. Revolutions arise out of collisions, through the contradiction which error carries within itself. Passions are the kernel of all revolutions, passions cause their outbreak. It is these passions which violently equalize once again those inequalities which have arisen out of themselves. When nature planted corruption in the breast of its children, it took care that it would only serve the goals of its existence by endowing it with the quality that it would in the end contradict and transcend [*aufheben*] itself. It goes without saying that we do not wish to excite blind passions by trying to contribute to the understanding of history.

There are two ways, however, of achieving the equalization of already existing inequalities. This can be reached by peaceful mediation or by violent battle. He who is clearly aware of the humane goals cannot opt for the latter, he cannot wish that equalization should be achieved by blind battle. This wish can be cherished only by those who do not know what they want, who are a blind instrument in the hands of Providence which reigns over the destiny of mankind as over everything else; or by those who have become aware of the humane goals, but have not yet seen sufficiently through the ways of Providence, ever guarding over us, to trust it.

Yes, Providence operates in two ways in order to reach its goal with mankind: the blind battle of passions, where like the opposing powers of nature which collide with each other, they fight among themselves and are then being overcome [*aufgehoben*]; and peaceful mediation through reason. Anyone who proceeds along the first route cannot then applaud the second one, because he has not yet reached consciousness, because he is himself still more or less blind or full of passions. He, however, who is committed to the second route, can equally not follow the first one, when the better way is closed to him – because he admits its faults and recognizes that it is only an emergency path and not the straight way to the goal.

(7)

Since all living is engulfed in constant progress, it is certainly much more advantageous for humanity to raise this progress to the level of consciousness than to be blindly subjected to it. The more people will be aware of their striving, the more humane their deed will become. They are less bestially blind, less cruel, the more their knowledge of God increases. The Holy Spirit of God teaches men to will what nature wills, to subject themselves to the Eternal Law, not to jeopardize their temporal and eternal salvation in a fruitless battle against nature and God.

Man's freedom consists not in his arbitrary will [*Willkür*], but in conscious obedience to the divine law. Obedience is the virtue of pure man. The pious child obeys without much fuss his superiors' authority; because its spirit is too weak to recognize the law. The pious youngster already feels, albeit darkly, what is right and what is wrong; he starts to search for it eagerly. Finally, the pious man has, through experience and diligent searching, recognized God's law; he pays homage to it through his conviction, out of free, inner impulse. The sinner, on the other hand, who lacks the divine light, who is not filled with the Holy Spirit, sets himself against the law because he has not received it within himself.

(8)

Therefore we are convinced that truth expressed dispassionately – the proclamation of the Eternal Law – even if it contradicts in certain respects the old established order (since like all temporal matters, it too is incomplete) – is still far from hurting order as such. Rather, according to our view, such expressions of truth contribute enormously to order itself, because they point to what is in tune with the times and what is not – because they reveal the will of God. After all, nobody denies that all living strives, consciously or unconsciously, towards perfection.

But so long as the state is still imperfect, yet lives and strives for perfection, collisions occur from time to time, and these have to be overcome. The representatives of the people's will – the governments – can therefore do nothing better for the maintenance of the social order than to encourage scientific enquiries relating to political life, in order to choose out of the results of this research that which avoids the collisions which emerge necessarily out of the period; because if these collisions are not mediated peacefully – namely through appropriate, new laws – they will in the end turn violently into revolutions.

We conclude these comments with a remark which every better author finds necessary in our time to add to his writings: that we shall not engage in the petty polemic which is still being taken up by some who presume to have a claim on scholarly education. Since we pay allegiance to our views not because they are necessarily ours but because they come from God or are true, we have an interest in defending them only as such. Therefore we can view the attacks of our opponents without passion and take pleasure in reporting, disseminating, and better grounding our views in so far as we increase our knowledge. The most vehement, fanatical, and malevolent attacks we can counter with the few words of that wise man who, in order to allay the blind zeal of the opponents of Jesus Christ, aimed at them the memorable words: 'If this counsel or this work be of men, it will come to naught; but if it be of God, ye cannot overthrow it' (Acts of the Apostles 5:38–9).

Written with the help of God, the Holy Spirit, on the Rhine, in the year of Christ one-thousand-eight-hundred-and-thirty-six.

Part Two
The Future, as the Consequence of what has Happened

It is not necessary that God himself should speak in order that we may discover the unquestionable signs of his will. It is enough to ascertain what is the habitual course of nature and the constant tendency of events. I know, without special revelation, that the planets move in their orbits traced by the Creator's hand.

TOCQUEVILLE[1]

FIRST CHAPTER

The Natural Striving of Our Age or the Foundation of the Holy Kingdom

You will wear Joy's splendid garment,
See the liar's brood destroyed.

SCHILLER[2]

---

[1] Alexis de Tocqueville, *Democracy in America*, trans. and ed. Henry Reeve and Francis Bowen (New York, 1963), I, p. 7.
[2] Friedrich Schiller, 'Ode to Joy', in *Immortal Lieder: 800 Years of German Poetry*, trans. E. Louisa Mally (Berlin, 1962), p. 78.

(1)

If the holy tradition is not a deceiver – if world history is and will be not a liar but the never-contradicting eternal truth, revealed in time as a logical conclusion – then we live at present in a period analogous to that of the deluge of water or the flood of the peoples. This analogy is important; it shows us the character of our era, its world-historical significance, with a certainty which one could not have reached through the previous points of view of historical research. As we find ourselves only called to proclaim the will of God in so far as our knowledge of Him determines our duties, so we shall seek to shed light only on what relates to our proximate future; but so as not to offer a truncated picture of world history, we shall mention the rest and leave its fulfilment to its own time.

(2)

What is most important for us is the striving to create new states, which we have also discovered in the two first periods after the rejuvenation; accordingly, even had we not found it amply established in the present, it would have followed from the comparison with the two known main periods. But in order to describe this striving more closely, we have to compare also something else. We have first of all to see what is generally the aim of all temporal endeavours and how it takes shape in relation to the social ordering of men; then we shall have to prove historically how it has to appear in our era, which has not yet reached the final goal [*Endzweck*] of society, but is on the way towards it. The latter is especially important: because it will be of little use for us to know the aim of humanity [*Bestimmung der Menschheit*], about which the philosophers have often kept us busy, when no light is shed on the way leading to it. Of what help is it to us to point to the light in the distance, if our steps are unsure because we are engulfed in darkness? Moreover, at night distances cannot be distinguished; and it is not rare to think that the light, towards which one strives, is already near when one is still miles away from it. Only world history can teach us about our standpoint – not world history as it has been conceived until now, but world history in its unity, totality, and necessity. Let us start our enquiry in this sense.

(3)

The general aim of all temporal striving is eternal truth, the one life, or God, to which all particular, one-sided, and partial life returns, as it has proceeded from it. Every particular striving is only a specific and definite form of this universality; therefore we find in things temporal this threefold life which we have designated as kernel, tree, and fruit. This law – proceeding from the kernel and then, enlightened or consciously, returning to the kernel as fruit, which finds itself again in the individual as well as in the whole – we have also discovered in human society, in the life of the totality of mankind viewed as a whole. The holy history of mankind presents us with the kernel of social order or the unity of humanity under the aegis of unconscious, unified life. This life begins internally with Adam as the original kernel; externally [it appears] as a visible root with Abraham, the ancestral father of the nation, in whose legislation the unity of life, or God, was unmistakably revealed. Because in the old bond everything is aimed at creating and maintaining unity and equality within the people – to create an alliance whose inner being is unity, or God, not an idol, and whose external form is equality, or liberty, and not any form of despotism. Therefore the [Mosaic] Law originally divided all goods equally among the people and saw to it that equality, so far as the conditions of the time allowed, would be maintained; without mentioning many other commandments, all of which had only this aim in mind – unity and equality.

(4)

But compared to our own time, the [Jewish] nation was then less aware of the divine Law, and thus squandered the gift with which Providence had endowed it. It showed itself still unworthy of this gift through the actions of its spirit and its consciousness. It has not yet recognized the value of the divine Law, because the knowledge of a good must first be mediated through its loss. The people behaved merely passively in accepting the Law through Moses, just as the human being receives his first life without actively seeking it. When, finally, mediated by much affliction, God appeared in Christ; when the divine Law, the unity of life, became revealed for the first time in the Son of Man; when man began to comprehend, albeit initially only darkly, but ever so strongly, what is right and what is wrong – then man made God, or God made man, finally broke through the narrow boundaries of nationality – just an a youngster breaks through the boundaries of family – and rose from the lowly terrestrial soil to the high goals of his destination towards universality and eternity.

The old bond was the kernel of social life; the fruit was to be the new bond of mankind. Jehovah, in so far as he was the God or the unity of the nation, had to yield to the God of humanity; so monotheism that visualizes God in images has to yield to ideal pantheism.

(5)

But just as all that is born in time also needs time for its development, so [it is] also with social life or the holy bond of humanity. Christianity represents social life in its growth, in its development; during it the old unity, the innocence of childhood, had to decline. Had mankind been highly educated right from the beginning, then it would not need education and formation [*Bildung*]. But the opposition which appeared now between spirit and matter, giver and receiver, became the death knell for what remained of equality among men: because now the conflict was that of man against man, and not – as in the time of germination – nature against man. On one hand, man was creator, giver, spirit; on the other, there were creation, what was received, nature. Power and dominion could appear during the time of growth and striving only in a one-sided way. We speak not only of the growth of the knowledge of God, of the inner striving of mankind, but also of its external struggle – of the striving of a young, powerful species which was the depository, in its early maturity, of a secret power which was dormant in it until now. That external and inner life go hand in hand has already been admitted; but that the totality of mankind, though we do not yet always recognize the inter-relationship, forms an internally connected whole, an individuum – this has not been recognized as such until now. The great event after Christ – the flood of peoples – provides an incontrovertible proof of this for anyone who can see; just as the deluge of water after Adam provides for any one who does not see it as a fable a proof that the life of mankind and that of the earth are likewise bound in an inner relationship.

(6)

When we said above that after Christ, unlike after Adam, not nature and man, but man and man got into conflict, then we meant neither the inner nor the external man – but both. The growth of social life from the lowliness of the old [Jewish] national bond to the height of humanity has been, like all growth, a crisis, a becoming. If a higher being was to emerge, the existence of the old holy bond had to decay, like that of all the ancient states which surrounded it. [Let us] emphasize once more the quintessence of social life – goods (and by this we do not mean exclusively the external ones); these could not have been distributed equally from the very beginning, because the receivers were not yet present, as they had to be found. For the same reason there could not have been a holy law, watching over unity and equality . . .

We have seen how Christianity has consummated its exalted course and how the kernel of the Holy Spirit finally emerged out of it. We have recognized that mankind started once more to return, internally and externally, to [its] kernel as fruit. We have further observed how culture turned from the Northeast to the Southeast, how it has wandered from one region of the world to another one. And mankind has begun again to turn into itself, to become united with itself – just as it had earlier burst outwards and broken the boundaries of the Law. We have recognized the general character of the current striving of mankind by recognizing the historical significance of the man who is the foundation of the new age; moreover, we have discovered not only the period, but not least the place, where the Holy Spirit has for the first time been revealed.

Once we have understood Spinoza and North America in their world-historical significance, no doubt can remain with us what our era wants in general – wants and will achieve . . . But we have also observed how the kernel of the Holy Spirit has seen the light of day, after it has grown in Europe internally for two centuries and has also been expanding from North America to our continent. Thus we recognize the necessity of our striving and growth not less than its form. In order to describe this more precisely, we would like to keep the kernel of our era closer in sight. Because the more we acquaint ourselves with the kernel, the better we shall come to know the fruit, which is nothing else than the kernel [made] visible.

(7)

The inner essence of all salvation is, according to the Master's teaching, the knowledge of God, the united consciousness of life. Accordingly, good is what promotes this knowledge; bad, by contrast, is what prevents or beclouds it. And because there is nothing for man in all of nature which promotes more his humane determination, the knowledge of God, than his brethren who are inspired by the same striving – it is further good that men associate, live in society. This is the teaching of the Master. He did not teach what should be, but what is: what is here in all eternity, this he merely brought to consciousness.

Once we have realized, according to this revelation, the primary cause which brings about our living in society; once we have recognized the unclouded consciousness of Eternal Life as the focus of the circle around which all our activity turns and rotates; once we have become aware of the goal of our strivings – then we shall never lose sight of this when we enter into a social association. We say: people who have become conscious of their striving after truth will, when they enter into a social association or renew one, make their arrangements is such a way that they will not harm the enjoyment of their true life, but put it to good use; such people will never again confuse means and ends.

Since men support each other only when they are inspired by the same striving, the social arrangements of those who have become aware of the humane goal will tend primarily to maintain their striving towards unity and equality.

(8)

But nothing can better correspond to the inner unity of spirits than harmonious cooperation. The harmony of external strivings necessarily supports and promotes the inner ones, and vice versa. The more the activity of one member provides for the benefit of the whole, and the richness of the whole benefits the individual, the deeper is the bond which binds the individuals with the whole and with each other. All separate beings constitute one being when the existence of the one is inconceivable without that of the other. Therefore unity and equality exist only when totality is present in everyone, and when everyone thrives and ripens through the other. This – namely, that inner and external harmony is the first condition of human society – we can discern also from the old [Jewish] covenant, as we have recognized it as the root of the great association of mankind. But it is enough to have drawn this from the Master's teaching, since we have equally comprehended it in its world-historical significance.

After we have, however, found that equality, external and internal, is the goal of our strivings, we still have to determine the degree of equality which is possible in our era. Because just as nature does not stand still, neither does it move in leaps.

(9)

Inspired people have already spoken much about the primordial equality of men; however, by this we have not yet become clearly conscious of our goal, because they have not brought history as their witness. Finally it has been asserted that the community of property [*Gütergemeinschaft*] is the goal of social life, but this statement has equally not helped us to proceed further. It is true that the turning point in the history of mankind has been crossed, that inequality has reached its peak and that with giant steps the road has been taken which leads downward to that plain in which there is room for all human beings.

Let us acknowledge the contribution of those who have pronounced the meaningful words 'community of property' – it has made us aware of the ultimate goal of social life. We speak therefore of those who have praised the community of property, in order to give them their due recognition. We maintain that 'community of property' describes most accurately and sharply the concept of 'equality'. The reign of full equality comes into being only where there exists communal ownership [*gemeinschaftlicher Besitz*] in all goods, internal as well as external, where the treasures of society are open to all and nothing is tied to a person as exclusive property.

Though we shall show in what follows that our aims are, for the time being, still far away from this ideal of equality, we do not belong to those who are scared by the right word, which nakedly describes the concept of a thing, and who would rather circumvent it by a pleasantly sounding meaningless phrase; we do not belong to those who have such a fear of real equality as of real death because the latter, as the former, destroys a phantom to which their life and their spirit are bound, and besides which they know nothing. Because just as our body developed over time and will eventually perish, so all inequality which emerged over time – including social inequality – will disappear in due time.

(10)

Yet all is still hidden from our eyes and shrouded in the thick fog of the future; and those people who, though unable to lift their veil yet nevertheless extremely keen on constructing hypotheses, do usually not hit the right point because they jump over it.

Our era strives towards equality – this cannot be denied; but [does this imply] that it is headed immediately towards community of property? Let this happen one day in the future, let it be the last goal of ageing mankind: we have already said that knowledge of the goal does not help us much, if we do not know the way [towards it]. Let us acknowledge our present point of view: we are concerned about our immediate future. Languages too will be united, just as they had been separated in the past. Just as the states must separate themselves according to their distinct tongues, though all are encompassed in a higher bond and can live in harmony – so an external community of property cannot come about before the spirits are re-united; and as we shall presently show this is so despite the fact that also when it comes to landed property harmony is both theoretically possible and can be implemented.

(11)

We turn to history and maintain that it is unnatural and atrocious to wish to abolish suddenly all inequality. Inequality had started before Abraham, namely when men started to separate and disperse; and just as they were split internally, so they also created distinctions between 'mine' and 'thine'. The apex of inequality has been mediated in mankind through the historical right. This began in the times of Abraham. After Abraham profit became inheritable! – since his descendants, as the holy history reports, have enjoyed his merits, the children without merit have inherited the great benefits of their ancestors.

And just as the Jews inherited the inner good, the knowledge of God, without having deserved it, so among the rest of the people of that epoch the external goods of heroic ancestors were transmitted through inheritance to degenerate sons. Since states have been established, the first ones who appeared as founders during the tribulations and confusions of the times had to excel in their virtues. But their descendants, on the other hand, who could live in quiet possession, in undisturbed enjoyment, who did not recognize the value of their goods, since they have not experienced how they had been acquired – they naturally became degenerates and wastrels. The truth of history regarding all temporal life, the tripartite existence, which re-appears in the individual as well as in the whole, had to be established also in social life, in the history of mankind.

Historical right has mediated the inequality of men, since their power increased one-sidedly and not equally any more. With the beginning of inheritance mankind started to be split into man and woman, into begetters and nourishers. A masculine and a feminine principle developed. The Jews, among whom the knowledge of God became inherited, represent the masculine principle, the pagans, among whom idolatry found its home, are the feminine.

(12)

The split in mankind had reached its height in the Christian period: this period was in every sense the era of blossom, the time of the youth of mankind. In it all contrasts appeared decisively in order to be reconciled for eternity – the contrast between masculine and feminine principles, between spiritualism and materialism. In the middle of the Christian era, the first matings began (one should compare the Crusader period). It was midnight – and the sun had passed its nadir and in a real sense day had already dawned, although it was still dark night. Before midday, before every distinction between light and darkness, male and female, spirit and matter, mine and thine could disappear, a long interval was still needed. The age of youth, morning's dawn, had to pass: only then could the beautiful time of maturity, which we have just approached, be experienced. It is only in old age, as in childhood, that all distinction between mine and thine can again disappear.

We should, however, rejoice in the point at which we now stand; we still do not want a community of property; our blood is still too hot for a life without action. We would like to act freely; we want an unrestricted freedom for our powers; through such activity we will and must earn the tranquillity of old age. It is a contrast: we would like to devour our winter reserve stock the moment autumn sets it. Has autumn really reached us? . . .

(13)

Historical rights have naturally to be abolished [*aufgehoben*] before that primordial equality of men can be restored. This primordial equality has to be mediated through the abolition [*Aufhebung*] of the right of inheritance, just as through the existence of inheritance the height of inequality is being mediated. Highest equality cannot emerge directly, as the [Saint] Simonists maintain, from Christianity, that peak of inequality. The striving of the contemporary world is encapsulated in the abolition of inheritance: it has already begun its work. But the culmination of its work still lies ahead; we still have to expect those who would really storm the heavens. Aristocracy has not yet received its final anointment . . . In order to understand more precisely what we mean to say it is necessary to delve deeper into the spirit of history.

(14)

In the beginning there existed natural equality among men; they were united because they were innocent, ignorant; because they knew only those needs which everyone could achieve easily without the help of others. Quarrels or collisions could not yet emerge among men, because their strivings were simple and uniform, and did not collide with each other in an unfriendly fashion. Though there was no harmony in their strivings, there existed equality – a primordial, natural equality. The enemies which they had to fight were not internal, and against the external foes each and all were strong enough.

This was the true kernel of society; these were men complete-in-themselves by nature. But later, as needs increased with the insight men gained into things; as the individual was no longer capable of satisfying them without the assistance of similarly inclined brethren; as imagination, tradition, speech, and customs [*Sitten*] multiplied; as the inner enemy – man – confronted man – then various artificial associations [*Verbände*] appeared. Men split apart, associated themselves in tribes, nations, empires. The right of inheritance emerged together with property: because the artificial associations of men, far from being perfect, were only preliminary attempts. Neither the general means of exchange – money – nor political economy were successful enough to guarantee the property of the members of the state without sanctioning the heritability [*Erblichkeit*] of goods. Free commerce and industry were still unknown – agriculture predominated: man was still shackled to the clod of soil. Besides, the sanctions of historical right were part of the spirit of the time. It would have been an enormous leap to proceed straight from the pure family life of the early human beings to a pure structure of a state which does not recognize any national or traditional differences [and acknowledges] only man as such. The early structures of the state had therefore to be patriarchal by nature, because they were akin to family life. Because the contours of the human face are a mirror which only reflects the image presented to it. The free human spirit was not yet developed, because man was not yet mature [*der Mensch noch nicht Mann war*], but a child who had to obey the authority of the elders.

(15)

The primordial equality of man disappeared with the progress of history, not because the law of property had been accepted, but because historical right accompanied it. Had the right of inheritance not followed in the footsteps of the right of property; had associations been possible in which the property of the members would, after their death, pass on not to their sons or to any other personal relatives, but to the state as the universality of life – and the state would then allocate to each citizen on his reaching maturity an equal portion out of its exchequer – then inequality would have been constantly equalized despite the existence of the right of property. But thus it happened that the more a state developed in time, the closer it approached its end; because this kernel of inequality grew into an inner split and finally culminated in full death. Hence in antiquity one state swallowed another, namely the younger the older, ultimately the last one all the preceding ones.

And as in the case of external goods, the same fate befell the inner ones. As the spirits split apart, with the different states there also appeared different religions. And because the knowledge of God became inherited by tradition within one people, which constantly brought together the dispersed spirits into unity, the distinction between holy and idolatrous religion became ever sharper up to that contradiction shown to us in its terribly sublime form by Rome as it turned spiritual. The earth was split into two parts: externally, the Northeast split away from the Southwest, just as internally spirit was divorced from body, spiritualism from materialism.

(16)

This is where freedom – life – came to an end and passed through death towards a higher life. This is how it was destined to be in the eternal plan of Providence; this is how it has to be according to nature. Conscious, human freedom had to be mediated through the loss of its pristine, unconscious freedom. Mankind had first to recognize what had been the origins of all its endless splits and divisions, all its internal wars, what was the source of every sort of bondage, of every kind of arrogance, of every injustice which had bedevilled it from the very beginning of its proper history since the emergence of historical right until the present day. It had first to find the source of its Fall, had to realize that every association, every social body, carried within itself the kernel of its own demise so long as the heritability of achievements pervades its arteries like some sneaking poison; it had to realize that the striving for a healthy, social constitution will remain futile so long as the fountain of inequality is not plugged. Only then would humanity be capable of recapturing its original, forfeited freedom and equality without losing it once more because of the old original sin. Mankind has to go through a long, unhappy school in order to reach this simple truth. But it was also a great, important lesson which had to be taught: the lesson how peace and freedom, how the highest bliss can be captured!

This lesson could not come from the outside, had to be reached through one's own experience. Only living history could be the class master here. Yes, history is a great teacher of humankind; this has been said often, though perhaps not always understood. History does not teach us what to do, but what to avoid; what we have to do, this is taught to us by the holy, creative Spirit.

We are faced with an inexhaustible repository of failed attempts; the most varied sorts of political constitutions have been tried and exhausted during the history of mankind; just as nature had to come closer from all sides towards its highest product before it could create its master work – man – so men strive in all possible ways towards the best constitution before they can reach the ideal of a holy covenant. It is reserved for us to recognize the foundations of the perfect holy state. History and philosophy call to us unanimously: there is no guarantee of the external harmony of life except through the inner one – and vice versa, just as spirit and body, freedom and equality, masculine and feminine always go hand in hand.

Never can the one arise at the expense of the other without bringing about its own death.

Our era, having become aware of this truth, will not forfeit this good, which it pursues consciously, once it has achieved it. This good it will soon achieve; no longer will it hunt for chimeras. The pursuit of material goods, which many look down on with the rapturous haughtiness of immature youth, is by itself not a sign of a dying, but of a strengthened spirit. We say that as such it is not an evil that our era pursues material goods: [it is evil] only inasmuch as this pursuit appears as egoistic, one-sided, inasmuch as it lacks the dedication to the common weal. But this egoism, this residue of inequality, digs its own grave. Soon it will be buried in the earth.

(17)

Harmony is the foundation of the holy kingdom, the goal towards which our era is striving: neither merely external [harmony], as the age is being reproached for, nor merely the inner one, as it is being imputed to it: but both. It is the task of our age to abolish [*aufzuheben*] the heritability of achievements, not to destroy the contrasts between individuals and nations, but – what will last enduringly – to bring them into an eternal concord.

Because we have to realize that universal life must in the end necessarily come to naught wherever there is an aristocracy, which concentrates the powers of society on one side while it pushes the other into humiliation and servitude. By this we do not mean that aristocracy whose power has already been broken, the aristocracy of the nobility, which has been attacked first because it stood in the way. We speak of the aristocracy of money.

(18)

Lerminier[3] has already remarked that in order to give a law extra power, its antiquity is being emphasized: but thus one only points out that it is approaching its demise. The author of the *Contrat Social* has explained to us this extraordinary fallacy: 'Why then is so much respect accorded to

---

[3] Jean-Louis-Eugène Lerminier (1803–57), French publicist and legal scholar.

ancient laws?' asks the upright Jean-Jacques, after having passed judgment about it more or less in Lerminier's vein. And he answers: 'Because society would have descended into anarchy, [since] in contrast, wherever the laws weaken as they grow older, it is proof that there is no longer any legislative power.'[4] Indeed! So long as no new laws are created, the old ones have to be honoured. Or as the old adage goes: don't pour out dirty water before you have clean. Yet this reasonable precept does not make the old law better; on the contrary, the old water becomes even more dirty and filthy the longer it is kept. If we wish to have fresh living water, we must eagerly look for it.

(19)

Since the age of the Patriarchs the belief dominated that when an individual dies, he does not return to the universal creator, to God, but to his ancestors. Fantasy confused the eternal with the temporal: it imagined the eternal with finite attributes, and the temporal with eternal ones. The same confusion endowed the right of inheritance, together with all its supplementary consequences, with its spiritual consecration. 'I at least cannot bow to the prejudice which grows out of the confused idea which maintains that because a man during his lifetime may dispose of his property as he wishes, he can maintain this privilege after his death. Because there is as much a difference between the rights of a living man and those of a dead one as there is between life and death.' We fully share this view which we have found in the English author. Bulwer.[5] But unlike that Englishman we would like to apply this not only to the old inheritance privilege of primogeniture, but to all old inheritance privileges of the family as well as to any relationship which does not encompass all of mankind. [We would like to apply this] to privileges which were timely during the age of the Patriarchs and in states which bordered on them [and had] patriarchal constitutions, but which are absurd in our age which becomes more distant from patriarchal life the more it approaches the pure life of the state. Our age has become aware that it is to eternal God – the great

---

[4] This is a paraphrase of a section of Jean-Jacques Rousseau's *Social Contract* in *Collected Writings,* ed. Roger D. Masters and Christopher Kelly (Hanover and London, 1994), IV, pp. 189f.

[5] No such quotation could be found in Henry Lytton Bulwer's *France: Social, Literary and Political,* first published in 1834 and subsequently translated into German, though Hess paraphrases here quite accurately ideas which appear frequently in Bulwer's work.

Whole – that the eternal law of inheritance belongs; that, by contrast, nothing can be possessed by individuals and nations in perpetuity since they are fleeting and limited.

(20)

Where the whole is alive, there all parts act harmoniously for the whole, not egotistically for themselves; in a fully developed individual no single faculty grows separately any more. The era of heritability is that of the growth and development of all faculties; with the arrival of maturity all development and inheriting cease. Through heritability all that is one-sided in mankind has arisen, as in nature: there death equalizes all differences – why should it not be the same here? Does not every member of the state, on attaining maturity, become a creditor of the state just as every individual becomes on birth a creditor of the universe? When this demands back, on the death of the individual, the capital which it has loaned him just for a limited period so that he could enlarge it – why should the state, on the death of its members, not demand back the capital which is basically its property?

We find in the old holy covenant an analogous maxim of this law. It stipulated that all property should revert after fifty years to its original owner (to whom it had fallen during the original, just distribution of property). Because the divine legislator considered all land as the property of the invisible national God [*Nationalgott*]: 'The land shall not be sold for ever', thus spoke Moses in Jehovah's name, 'for the land is mine; for ye are strangers and sojourners with me' (Leviticus 25:23).

Obviously the same truth, which would bring about harmony in the life of the state in times in which free commerce and industry predominate, caused only a limited uniformity when agriculture still formed the main source of subsistence. Truly we do not find in all of history an example out of which the kingdom of God could be constructed as a worthy model; because until now, mankind has not yet been fully formed. As pointed out, history shows us the limitations and excesses of our childhood and young adulthood. It is in nature that we discern a worthy image of full human maturity, and it is from it that we should learn.

The earth is fully developed – not so young as to indulge in excesses, not so old as to have already become rigid, inert, and powerless; it is in its best years – we should emulate it, because we too enter into our best years. [The earth] does not teach equality, community of property;

it is mountains, trees, flowers, animals, and human beings that actively swarm before the eyes of the beholder; but it does teach harmony – the highest living creatures must serve, after their death, the lowliest ones, and the latter during their lifetime [serve] the higher. The death of the animal kingdom is the life of the plant kingdom, and that in its turn serves the life of the former. Similarly, the death of the talented, affluent part of society will enrich the life of the property-less; and, as once before, the untalented will again have to support the talented.

One should not object that human society will not be able to imitate the divine arrangements. Why should it not, when it has in its way arrived at the level of its great teacher and mother? The same God who reigns over the earth and over nature is also active in history – there universally, unconsciously; here individually, consciously.

Or has the financial system not been puzzled out sufficiently to be able to construct out of itself an artificial economy equal to the economics of nature? Can the financial calculations not be applied equally to simple, benevolent aims just as to the most intricate and corrupt machinations? We do indeed know that certain people have many objections to God's arrangements; but we are not called to respond to this. The wheel of time will roll over these anthills without causing any damage.

In any case, let those who have only their own advantage before their eyes lament, together with the cowards and short-sighted in their retinue, the decline of the old social order and thus believe that barbarity and anarchy will, as after Christ, break out again. Yet we say that the true life of the state will begin when the historical right is abolished. Only then will mankind reach the height of its earthly bliss. Each age reaches its bliss when it lives through its course naturally; but the fullness of bliss resides in maturity, and it is not in vain that these years are called the best. But we have to make ourselves better understood.

(21)

The son inherits the father on his death; the daughter receives a dowry when she leaves the paternal household, so she can start her own. This is how is has been everywhere from time immemorial, ever since men have left the state of nature in order to come closer through social associations to their humane goal, the knowledge of God. This has been so, we say, since men congregated together in order to support each other; this is how it has been from the North to the South Pole, in the American democracy as well as in Chinese despotism. We repeat: it has been and is like that everywhere and in all times: but wherever and whenever it has been like that, it had its good reason to have been and be like that . . . *In the future it will not be like that among us, because it has no justification.* Where the cause disappears, the consequences also vanish: the house that stands on an undermined and groundless foundation will collapse in a terrible clatter if it is not dismantled in good time and rebuilt on firm ground.

(22)

Since Christ the old basis of the social order has been undermined and rebuilt at the same time on a new foundation: equally the principle of nationality sank as that of mankind arose. The Christian era, the Middle Ages, has been, as we know, a transition period from the old order to the new; Christendom lived in the hope for a future kingdom of truth, a New Jerusalem. These hopes, engendered by Christianity, are close to their fulfilment – partly, they have already been fulfilled. We have once pointed out to those timid [people], who look back to the old caterpillar status, because they have been denied the free vision of the future (Part I, §41). Those who have no trust in God because they do not know his ways are afraid of any new step. They tremble before every reform, before every new stone which they should lay into the foundation of the social edifice to replace an old, weathered one. Because they fear that the house may come tumbling down on their head. What cowards! They do realize that it cannot remain as it is; they know quite well that the old debt is great and is being doubled every moment – but they would like to continue to maintain the dignity and honour of the house through miserable palliatives. Why do they not think of the future – about the growing corruption that if not today, then tomorrow, will unavoidably bring about the collapse? Why do they pile debt upon debt rather than think of a total cancellation [of all debts]? But they are blind because of their passions, and like an animal can think only of the present moment. We shall overlook these proud cowards, who are incapable of responding to reason and prefer to boast in words rather then admit their situation openly and honestly. They may continue to delude themselves as well as others – – – History will judge.

(23)

Our institutions have lost their foundation and basis. Because they have been anchored in the limited human spirit, which was incapable of protecting personal property without diminishing human achievement; [it was incapable] of maintaining the order of the whole without impinging on the liberty of the individual, of sanctioning obedience without glorifying the feeling of blind authority, of strengthening sociable bonds without instituting the enslaving chains of matrimony, of increasing the activity of man without the impulse of lowly egoism, of praising the hero without encouraging the spur of ambition, of worshipping self-effacement without the hope of reward in the hereafter, of conveying the consciousness of eternity without a sensuous image of temporal permanence – and of propagating the knowledge of God without a mercenary priesthood.

But all these goods, without which no society can endure, will be present – but without their poisonous admixtures. Yea, without them the property of persons will be so much better protected than heretofore, the order of the state maintained in a less distorted way, the law observed ever more piously, the bonds of society ever more strongly tied together, the heritage of those coming of age more substantial, manly activity greater, the heroes' courage more determined, the readiness to make sacrifices for the good of the whole more frequent, the belief in eternity livelier and the glory of God ever greater! And all this – because the kingdom of truth is upon us, because the Holy Spirit has been set free. This Spirit will easily perform what to us still appears as wondrous; because its quiet power is far stronger than the noisy wonder powers of previous times.

SECOND CHAPTER

Our Present Plight as the Mediator of the Foundation of the Kingdom

Thou fool, that which thou sowest is not quickened, except it die.
                                    1 CORINTHIANS 15:36

(24)

In the previous chapter we discovered the foundation of the Kingdom of God. We found that it resides in the harmony of the strivings of those who take part in the holy kingdom. We saw that this harmony comes about primarily through the total abolition of the historical right, which brings about also other reforms. But easy as it is to pronounce this, the more difficult will it be to carry it out. We should not conceal that the foundation of this kingdom will be mediated through a great plight which we are about to encounter. It is our duty to bring this plight to our consciousness, to mitigate it through understanding. Because, little hope as there is that the collision facing us can be mediated peacefully, we should not refrain from contributing according to our ability towards overcoming this split. Our vocation is to promote salvation through understanding and reason. Woe be to us if we should be deterred by any sort of passion from following this divine vocation!

(25)

By comparing the two main periods of history we already recognize that the plight confronting us will consist in a great confusion of ideas as an outcome of the revolution of the spirit. But a closer knowledge of it has to proceed from recognizing its causes, which are especially active in our era. It is these that we have to examine.

We have already recognized the cause of all social woes in the inequality of men, which emerged after the Fall. We have further recognized that the origin of inequality has to be looked for in the development of the right of property in so far as it has been accompanied by the heritability of achievements. Yet the specific causes which have formed this evil in a given place in distinct and peculiar forms can be found only where the given and specific outcomes become apparent. Sin and evil are as much faithful companions as virtue and bliss; but just as no particular and specific bliss has ever been explained through the general concept of virtue or godliness, which we define as unclouded consciousness united-in-itself – so no particular evil can be understood through the general recognition of sin or godlessness, which we designate in relation to any life as division, disharmony and inconsequence.

(26)

As we have seen, the inequality of men reached its height in the middle of the medieval age. And it is from this time that it began to decrease. Yet it is false to see because of this the inequality of the Middle Ages – as it is still done frequently nowadays – as the cause of our inequality. One usually reproaches the knighthood or the aristocracy of the Middle Ages for the fact that the people live today in oppressive class differences [*Standesverschiedenheit*]. The time has however come to exonerate the medieval nobility from the guilt with which it had once been not unjustly burdened, but from which it has in our times been mostly cleansed. The time has come, we say, to turn from blind zeal to reason, since reason has triumphed. We have to grant the opponent the fullness of justice, once we have prevailed over him. Let us finally be gentle and fair towards the nobility, since it has been disarmed.

If we seek the nobility in its sphere in which it truly lived – in the Middle Ages – we find it altogether free from all guilt. If one can at all make one part of society responsible for what has been proved to emerge by necessity in any given period, then we would call to task the masses of the people rather then the noble lineages as bearing the guilt for medieval serfdom. The mass of the people, which acquiesced in such lowly slavery, had justly to bear the consequences of its slave-like consciousness until it rose once more to virtue. It was not the courageous knights, who soared upward and divided among themselves the spoils, who were responsible for the inequality of the estates [*Stände*], but the lower orders, who did not tear it away from them. Since the latter felt themselves comfortable in their lowly standing; since they were not filled with the glowing desire to raise themselves to higher levels – then we confusingly ascribe our views, the ideas of a better era, to these slaves [and] feel compassion for their oppression which they themselves did not feel. Men who do not see themselves of equal rank are, in fact, not [equal], and no injustice is done to them if they are treated as serfs.

The people are a large mass of power, therefore the origins of its submission cannot be the superiority of external force, nor an accidental superior cunning of its oppressors; what is at work here is an inner, spiritual weakness, combined with a baseness of the soul as compared to the spiritual strength and greatness of soul of the rulers. The external slavery of a people can never last longer than its inner, than its consciousness of being slaves [*Sklavensinn*].

(27)

Those who have been favoured by the mere accident of birth have willy-nilly given up the prerogatives which had once befallen them through their ancestors: they realized that the foundation for these privileges has disappeared. When we turn our attention to the behaviour of the nobility in recent times, then we find examples in which it has given back, in a truly noble way, what it had inherited and what it had claimed by historical right. Often it gave up its privileges – now turned illegal, once having been lawful and legitimate – even in circumstances in which it still had nasty means of defence under its control. And where it resisted the demands of the age, there it has been forced into obedience by the heroes of the age.

Now, after the Frankish[1] wars – after Napoleon – little is left of the old nobility besides the name; its pride as well as its power have been broken. Yet when we plead for the defence of the nobility, we do not intend to say that the last remnants of the external privileges should be kept at a time in which their inner foundation has disappeared. But we would like to turn the core of our power away from an opponent who is already in flight, in order to aim it at another one, whose power is increasing.

---

[1] Hess uses here several times the slightly derogatory *fränkisch*, instead of *französisch*, which is the term he uses on other occasions.

The nobility is no longer the enemy who can destroy our future – rather, it is the rich; yes, the rich have become the enemies of progress, and will become so even much more [in the future]. The aristocracy of money will show as much obstinacy as was once shown by the nobility when the battle was waged against it in the matter of historical right. The moral as well as the physical misery which begins to rule now is caused by the growing richness of one part of society as well as by the increasing poverty of the other. This disharmony, this inequality, this egotism will increase even further. The better and more insightful [people] already complain of this social malady. But it will reach such heights that it will frighten even the most obtuse and obstinate ones . . .

(28)

Money is the only lever of society once free commerce and industry have become dominant; and the greater their progress, the more powerful it becomes. This power will however become divine when inheritance is abolished – but will remain devilish, so long as it exists. And it is to this money-devil [*Geldteufel*] that man becomes more and more beholden when he does not live in a holy covenant and has neither fatherland nor family. The old laws are constantly being violated, therefore confusions and contradictions abound. This contradiction, which emerges because the customs and laws appear to be in transition, will further increase the more history develops.

(29)

Once Christianity has ceased to give life its blessing, and the idea of the fatherland, the enthusiasm for the common weal, which has been sanctified in antiquity, could not find new roots; once the pure life of the family has long vanished, but the pure life of the state [*Staatsleben*] has not arisen; finally, once that first sign of life of the New Age, which during the Frankish Revolution flashed like a meteor across the sky of mankind, has been extinguished and continues to glimmer only in the depth of the most noble souls – those priests of the age, who guard the holy fire – then public life has once again become bereft of its noble driving force, just as it had been in the recent previous period between the Peace of Westphalia and the French Revolution.

Once again we have no God, no holy kingdom, no religion, and no fatherland! Except the few who are nourished at the breast of science – besides also the holy martyrs of our age – there is only materialism, gross selfishness. This, however, is no wonder, only its opposite. Does there exist in our age any activity, except the purely scholarly, which is not motivated by the most coarse egotism? Is there anyone who is active who is aware of not working [merely] for his transient 'I'? Who can say with certainty that his diligence will benefit mankind, that he is active for the universal, that he works for the eternal by being productive? No one! Because no one works within a holy covenant. The fruits of our labour are surrendered up to blind chance and accident; there is no law that guarantees that once we are not here any more, they will revert to our brethren and sons.

It is not that all are active for each, and each for all: it is each for himself, as among animals. But it is a conscious life of animals: we recognize our baseness; we know that each has his claws and teeth so as to tear apart and devour his brethren for his own survival. We know that our peace has evaporated, that our life has become an inner struggle, that humanity has disintegrated. We have been torn away from Nature, do not lie any more at the breast of the all-nourishing mother; but our sight is not yet straight, directed upwards to heaven. We are dependent upon ourselves, but have not yet discovered our inner treasure. We have organs for gorging ourselves [*Fressorgane*], but no organs for thinking. Our innocence has been lost such a long time ago that we recognize our guilt: yet this does not help us at all.

Working for the public good has become a ridiculous phrase, an echo from ancient times about which hypocrites boast; yet for the better ones it is a mere memory of a long-lost spirit! And since Christian mysticism has also outlived itself; since few can lift themselves to Christ, because time has lifted the veils behind which the God of the Christians has been honoured: what is thus left to us is nothing else than the empty skull of a vain self-seeking which goes on living in order to feast, to booze, to whore, to shine – in short, which loves everything else, and lives for everything else – but for the purely humane and divine!

One should not object [by saying] that the same conditions had existed in the past. At that time, external conditions – in antiquity, and especially in the Middle Ages – were much worse than ours; consequently the inner conditions were in accord with them; this is not the case with us – and this is the great evil of our time. We have become men of reason, human beings which will not be dazzled by fantasy or lulled to sleep by feelings. The old ideas have disappeared; woe be to us so long as new ones do not appear in their stead and the disparity between our inner clear mental outlook and our external turbid external life endures!

(30)

In our time wealth is being derived according to its nature not through robbery, not as in former times through the impoverishment and oppression of other people: [nowadays] it increases not externally, but internally. The Holy Spirit subjugates the forces of nature, not human power. Therefore the fact that our era is confronted by a major affliction has not been caused by the pursuit of material goods. The nature of this pursuit attests much more to an expectation of a higher bliss; it provides the proof that it does not fit our point of view, and that it is solely due to our obsolete laws that we still have helots. According to the way our laws and institutions are currently operating, the new inventions of mechanics, the daily rising industrial and commercial activities, serve only to increase inequality, to enhance the wealth of one part [of society] and the poverty of the other.

It is obvious that the new inventions, as well as the daily increase in commerce and industry, are nothing else than an instrument in the hands of Providence of promoting harmony and the realm of truth; because they push the contrast between wealth and poverty to its peak – and then this contrast must be equalized. But woe betide us if this contrast will not be mediated peacefully but will be adjusted through a revolution!

Let us not conceal from ourselves our own evil, let us not fool ourselves! Let us not dream any more with that Englishman, whom we have already mentioned in these pages, of 'the rule of the middle classes'[2] so long as inheritance has not been abolished! In our age, at a time when the material power of man has been replaced by that of nature; when the constricting coercive power of guilds and corporations must yield before unlimited stock-holding companies; when every middleman and every craft must give way to wholesale business and industry – at a time, we say, in which free commerce and industrial activity finally swallow up every individual activity into a universal maw – at such a time the middle class must

---

[2] The reference is to Bulwer, *France*.

constantly further decline if the unequal distribution of goods will not equalize itself on its own.

If such an equalization does not occur, then we shall see even in countries in which at the moment goods are still divided more equitably, e.g. in France and North America, that the contrast between rich and poor will appear even harsher than in England, where an unequal distribution of goods has existed since long ago. We mean to say that such countries in which the collision between rich and poor is presently mediated, yet no provision has been made for the future, have only a meagre advantage when it comes to [questions of] the inequality in the distribution of goods.

Such collision cannot be mediated through any laws which have merely agriculture in mind. Such laws, which might have achieved their aim in ancient times, are relegated in our age to the role of mere palliatives, with which we are richly endowed; since nowadays it is not agriculture, but commerce and industry that predominate. Only when the harmony of pursuits is established among men can the external wealth, which issues from the internal one, have a reciprocal impact on it and promote the knowledge of God. Only when money ceases to be the devil can there be God.

(31)

Where unity reigns, there is power, life, freedom. With discord weakness sets in, death, serfdom; with it life ceases and passes to another one through death. Our era is such a period of transition.

After the wars of religion of the seventeenth century the kernel of the New Age was laid; after the political [wars] of the nineteenth century it was released; after the confusions which we confront, it will appear independently as a root. And the mother will die off and become rigid; but it will survive and bear fruit.

We have pointed out the essential conditions for the emergence of the holy kingdom, so that nobody should be mistaken about the redemption of the age and come to grief out of ignorance. We have shown that it is not to be looked for in the form of government; that the social plight is deeper, that it lies in the heritability of achievements, in the so-called historical right, in the aristocracy – not in the dying one of the nobility, but in the rising one of money. Let him who has ears – hear! - - -

(32)

In the heart of Europe will the New Jerusalem be founded. Germany and France are the two extremities of East and West – the extremes out of whose meeting the divine fruit will arise. Because the character of the French is the opposite of that of the Germans – the former is to be designated as political, the latter as religious. The interest in political-social problems is common to the French; the German bond, however, is a spiritual need, a religious-social moment. The French are as little united in their political views as the Germans are in their religious opinions; in France it is politics, in Germany religion, which is at the root of divisions and parties.

Germany was and remains the land of the great religious battles, just as France is the land of the world-historical, political revolutions. The nature of these wars teaches us however about the character of these two nations, because one does not quarrel over something in which one is not interested. As all high life can be mediated only through the death of a lower one, so truth can see the light of day only through the friction of different opinions, through doubt. Because truth is not the destruction, but rather the uniting of different opinions or mistakes: therefore these have not to be ignored with indifference, but have to be fought through with enthusiasm; only thus will a wholesome idea result.

Therefore we say: from France, the land of political battles, will true politics set forth one day, just as true religion will proceed from Germany. It is through the union of both that the New Jerusalem will emerge. And the trumpet of the age will sound for the third time, and the kingdom of truth will be founded.

THIRD CHAPTER

The New Jerusalem and the End of Days

> Then cometh the end, when he shall have delivered up the
> kingdom to God, even [to] the Father; when he shall have put
> down all rule and all authority and power.
>
> I CORINTHIANS 15:24

(33)

After the plight comes to a head, the kernel of the Holy Spirit will turn
into a stem and the word of the Master into a deed. The age will then
appear in all its glory and life will be One again and the lost peace will
be here once more. It is not our purpose to follow the ages in detail,
but we have to provide a general overview of them, so that the picture of the holy history will not be mutilated but appears as a whole,
albeit only as a mere sketch. But how can we dare to describe our future
without being filled with divine passion? Let therefore nobody consider
the following as a mere figment of our fantasy. It is like all that preceded it the fruit of mature reflection, and if it appears in the garment of
poetry, so this is so because in the period ahead of us ideal and actuality
[*Wirklichkeit*] are one; actuality becomes ideal, because the ideal is being
actualized.[1]

---

[1] This is a clear allusion to Hegel's key statement in his *Philosophy of Right* that 'What is rational
is actual, and what is actual is rational' ('*was vernünftig ist, ist wirklich, und was wirklich ist, ist
vernünftig*'). See *Hegel's Philosophy of Right*, trans. T. M. Knox (Oxford, 1948), p. 10. The
revolutionary potential inherent in this statement has become the foundation of the radical
interpretation of Hegel as presented by the Young Hegelians.

(34)

In the holy kingdom politics will be founded on holy, eternal principles, cared for by the pious and the loyal. The rulers and the ruled, made into one, will live in a concord freed from strife, encountering each other in a brotherly fashion; they will not have to conceal their inner sentiments. And the Kingdom of God will no longer seek conquests; its only aim will be to promote humanity [*Humanität*]. Where it will be unable to spread it, where it will be unable to make men into the brothers and comrades-in-bliss; where it will not be able to accept individuals and nations into its covenant – there it will limit itself to defence, until they will be ready to become citizens of the kingdom. Thus it lays claim to the highest advantage of the perfect state, which the citizens of the Kingdom of God will know.

The country will be internally united and externally strong, because everyone will dedicate all his faculties to the fatherland. And in the heart of the country there will be no citadels with their towering battlements and constricting walls. Villages will adorn themselves with wonderful buildings and cities with inspiring gardens; the whole country will become one large garden, in which a lot of happy and industrious people will be moving about and enjoying life, as befits human beings. Misery will be sought out, so that it can to be alleviated, but little will be found; misfortune will have taken its leave from man. Man will not longer labour in the sweat of his brow, but will earn his bread in free and cheerful zest for life; and woman will be equally freed from the curse and share life's full joy with man. Youth, educated in public schools in accordance to its nature, will jump bravely into life like a young foal; and cared-for old age, in the blissful fullness of manly activity, will return home to a living, known, eternal God!

(35)

Woman will enjoy the same humane education as man. And man and woman will be united through the bond of free love. And the education of the young will take place under the direct and immediate supervision of the state. No more will it be left to chance whether the parents, according to whether they are reasonable or stupid, rich or poor, educate their children to be human or non-human [*Unmenschen*]. Chance and arbitrary accidentality will no longer have access to the social relations of men;

every individual will enjoy the protection of the divine law. No longer will youth be subject to the arbitrariness of parents or guardians, woman to that of man, the poor and the weak to that of the wealthy and strong.

(36)

Matrimonial bondage [*Ehezwang*] as currently existing will disappear in the holy kingdom; the bonds of marriage will no longer be enslaving chains. In the place of forced submission will come free devotion. The loved ones will be able to be united without being prevented from the highest and noblest joy of life by haughty or avaricious parents or guardians. Man will no longer need to turn to venal persons in order to satisfy basely his noblest pleasure, and virtuous woman will no longer wilt in her prime.

The idea of free love is not new, it had been articulated long ago; but in the Kingdom of God it will be realized. In an era in which blind faith, based on authority, disappears, all laws which are based on it have to lose their force. Therefore the laws of matrimony, like all similar laws, will disappear in the holy kingdom. Before Christ, woman was a naught; in the Orient she is still now a slave. Christ has prepared her emancipation; in the Kingdom of God it will be full!

(37)

At the same time the state will replace the family and conduct the education of the young. Worthy men have raised objections to this; this will not, however, change the course of history, because patriarchal, pure family life and humane, free political life [*Staatsleben*] exclude each other. Until now history has merely presented the transition from the one to the other; ours is still a mixture of family and political life. But the closer we come to the pure life of the state, the further we move from pure family life. That this is a high ideal, a situation of laudable pursuit, will be admitted by any one who has a worthy notion of it. That mankind is however not yet ripe for this and can be led to this pure life of the state only through stages – this will be admitted only by those who have conceived the history of mankind in its totality.

The patriarchal, pure family life is the last – as well as the first – condition of mankind, mediated through the humane, pure life of the state. Humanity cannot yet return to the innocence of patriarchal life. Only in mankind's old age, when it shall recover its pristine innocence, will family life reappear, as in its childhood, in its purity. When the time arrives when men will no longer need to live under an external law, because each will carry the law in his own heart – when the pristine innocence of mankind, raised through time to self-consciousness, returns – then, as in the beginning, every parental pair may found its own state. We, however, who have not yet landed at this stage of perfection, will have to be content with the position assigned to us. We are assigned to the pure life of the state, and will therefore have to forgo the pure family life, which is incommensurate with our customs; because the declamations of well-meaning philosophers and poets can as little resurrect what has been destroyed in the course of time as can be achieved by external laws from time immemorial. Once the spirit has gone out of the old form of family life, mankind has only two alternatives: pure political life – or anarchy. Yet it is order, and not anarchy, which is the goal of history as well as of nature, and even if the latter is mediated through the former, it still remains the purpose and goal!

(38)

In the holy kingdom there will be no contradictions. Laws which can not be implemented universally and consistently like truth itself – those miserable palliatives, which one encounters in periods of transition and supply the sinner with a cover, but constrain the freedom of the pious – such [laws] will cease to exist in the Kingdom of God. Nor will there be any form of personal bondage, which necessarily degenerates into arbitrary rule so long as the human individual does not yet carry the law of God internally and needs no external commandments. Mature man will no longer revel in unattainable ideals. The pious, insightful parental pair who recognize the will of God will joyfully leave its children in the care of the state which – because it protects them – has rights over them. It will not be a heavy sacrifice for the mother to dedicate the fruit of her womb to God, to whom she and her children owe their better existence. Woman's greatest fame will be to give healthy, strong children as a present to the state – just as man's pride will consist in rendering to the state's exchequer the richest fruits of his labour. The noble consciousness to work not for his transient 'I' alone, but to do so within a holy covenant with humanity, will ennoble his life passion and comfort him on his deathbed.

And liberty will produce in woman, as well as in man, a purely human patriotism, which will be not less strong than that which had prevailed in antiquity. And unlike the Spartan, the citizen of the Kingdom of God will be educated not only to renounce, but also to enjoy – yet will be incomparable in his renunciation!

(39)

Society will have such an indescribable abundance of faculties, that it will do wonders. Nothing will appear impossible for the state, because it will no longer be dependent upon the egoism of its members; and the members will be able to move about freely and full of energy, because they will no longer be constrained by an anxious chief, but will be supported by the whole; each will unfold his highest activity, because one will no longer get in the way of the other.

The interests of the rulers and the ruled, of officials and citizens, will blend into each other; the cooperation of all in the state machinery – like the universe, so highly articulated yet so simple – will be so harmonious, and this harmony so manifest and obvious, that no patriotism of any state in antiquity would equal that of the new league of nations (*Völkerbund*). In this new Holy Covenant religion and politics will be once again one – a unity of which the states of antiquity provide us merely with a weak example. The Kingdom of God will lack neither means nor goodwill to develop the most useful institutions: health institutes of all kinds for the welfare of fools and sinners, of the weak and the sick, of all who need help and suffer from want. No longer will mankind have to kill out of love, like savages, those of its members for which it has no use; no longer will it have to obey barbaric customs in order to avoid barbarity, to punish in order to reform. Mankind will not have to deny its compassion to those who err; it will re-educate those who in old age have become dependent again . . . And the needy and the criminals will decrease every day, because men will gather strength in body and spirit . . .

(40)

Finally, what can then be said of the constitution of a commonwealth in which intelligence reigns supreme and all are free and equal? Nature and history lead to the same results – history does this in a negative way. In antiquity – so history teaches us – the body of the people predominated; its political form reached its perfection in democracy. In the Middle Ages, it was the soul, the heart of the people; in the aristocracy, the political age reached its apex. In the modern age the people, according to the law of the time, once again achieves domination: but not the body, the masses – it is the spirit of the people [which will rule]; its political form will reach its perfection in the representative institutions. Nature supplements history, shows us a positive result. The people – so it teaches us – is the pristine element [*Urelement*], the substance, the God and the Lord, whose life or consciousness, by individuating or universalizing itself, creates an organized whole, a living individual.

Every community will constitute, like a heavenly body, a world unto itself; but the different communities will live in eternal harmony, since they are subject to a higher order which as the unity of consciousness constitutes the mainspring which determines, orders, and guides their reciprocal relationships. This higher world – the state – shall, in so far as there will exist in the Holy Kingdom separate states or nations, be subordinated to the unity of consciousness of all states, just as the communities are subordinated to the state. Head and heart, the spirit and the soul of the people (we mean the legislative and executive power) will not be separated artificially – a separation in which until now one has not unjustly been seeking a salvation. Because when contrasts prevail, balance has to be sought; but when harmony rules, there is no need for an artificial construct, only a natural simplicity. There harmony had first to be created, here it has only to be preserved.

Just as in organic nature the nerves draw their nourishment from the blood and control and guide it for the benefit of the whole, so in the Holy Kingdom the legislators will be recruited from the executors of the law, from the officials, and control and guide them. The officials will be the mediators between head and trunk, between the spirit and the body of the people.

(41)

Who would need a Charter, an external law for the whole, when the law lives in its interior? What abuse can be carried out through a power which is restrained by nature? Which perfidy can take place in a commonwealth where everything is open and public, where free judgment is being recognized as the element of life? In eternal youth, in permanent freshness the laws will proceed from the head, and no injurious [laws] could emerge, because all interests are interwoven. Because the old contrasts between the low and the high, plebeians and patricians, the poor and the wealthy – this source of all collisions, disturbances, iniquities, and horrors – these have all lost their poison in the holy kingdom; contrasts are no longer dangerous in the Kingdom of God, because they equal themselves out in a natural fashion: they become weaker by the day, and in the end they must cease altogether.

Therefore the form of government – that power which has to watch over the laws, defend and execute them – will be determined every time from above, according to the needs of the moment, by the legislators. Thus the mass of the people will be ruled and guided by the government – and the latter will be controlled by the people's intelligence. There will be three powers in the Kingdom of God: the people as a mass – or the body of the people; the people as the executor of laws – or the will of the people; and finally, the people as legislator – or the spirit of the people.

We conclude these pages by summarizing what has been said and add some indications about what will happen in later times in order to present a simple, living idea of the holy history of mankind.

(42)

As the time of the old covenant, founded by the first revelation, came to an end, mankind was released from the old Law through the second divine revelation. The old states had a patriarchal constitution; man still stood in the background; only the member of the folk and the tribe [*Volks- und Stammgenosse*] was recognized by the law. Their mental horizon was limited, as no Christ had yet arisen to enclose mankind within his divine Spirit.

Rome constituted the transition from the old states to the new large external commonwealth of nations in a spatial sense; a little later Christ constituted the same transition, based on the foundations laid out by Rome, in a spiritual sense. Originating in Judaism, which had recognized the unity of God, Christianity was the masculine principle which developed now, detached itself from the feminine, in order to be wedded to it again. The Christian era – the Middle Ages – constituted the transition of mankind from boyhood to maturity. In that era religion – the spiritual, masculine principle – detached itself from politics, the feminine, spatial principle. Because if the old life, the old unity, was to evolve into a new and higher one, it had to be split. The old being had to decay; the church had to be separated from the state. In this great period of transition one could not imagine a divine law, a religious politics, a political religion; because the law was in the state of becoming.

(43)

Judaism was an absolute entity, complete unto itself, appearing spiritualist when compared to paganism, yet materialist when compared to Christianity. Mosaic legislation referred both to the inner as well as to the external man. Religion and politics, church and state were intimately blended, possessed one root, bore one fruit. The Jews did not know a distinction between religious and political commandments, between what is due to God and what is due to Caesar. These and other distinctions disappeared in the face of the one Law, which did not care for the body or the spirit alone, but for both.

The Gospels, on the other hand, related solely to the inner man; in Christianity, religion became divorced from politics. The Christians did not possess a social order founded on God; [they had] no holy state, no divine Law. But Christ felt in his divine soul the approaching anarchy and preached resignation before the will of God. The Man-God had a presentiment that a long, great plight would have to mediate the welfare of mankind and therefore suggested surrendering to the will of Providence, finding solace in the hope for the Holy Spirit. Of the resignation which Christ taught, he gave himself a living example, an example which shines throughout history more than all words, and makes it possible to recognize the world-historical significance of Christ. The death of Christ is the greatest wonder, the unmistakable sign of his divine mission.

Jesus Christ was the light that shone brightly through the darkness of the Middle Ages. He cleansed Providence from a heavy guilt in the eyes of weak men. He was the first to suffer judicial murder in the holy state without feuding with God, because he had already felt how out of the death of the lowly, terrestrial life of fantasy a higher, eternal life will proceed. He was the spiritual representative of that intensive middle period which was to follow him.

The suffering of Christ was the model for the suffering of mankind – in it mankind's higher significance became revealed. Christ has suffered for mankind inasmuch as he served as a divine example of how to save humanity through belief, love, and hope – even under the axe of the executioner, under the Cross. The spirit of Christ is immortal. As long as it is possible for violence or guile to murder virtue with impunity, so long will the religion of Christ, the power of his teaching and his example, be felt as a living example. Jesus Christ is the focus of history, the heart of mankind; his blood will pulsate in its veins so long as it endures. The belief in Christ will never die, because so long as the world prevails, individual cases, certain times and places will bear witness to his truth.

But not always, and not everywhere, will these gloomy cases predominate: naked force and false cunning will not be victorious forever. In the second revelation the old Law was lost; the third will introduce a new one. The time approaches in which the unity, which has been destroyed in the Whole, will be restored, when the state will become holy once more, when the Kingdom of God will reappear. Because out of the dead of the old life, new life comes forth.

The old Law was crucified together with Christ only in so far as it had been external, existing in time and space; but its divine content, its eternal spirit, continued to live, conquered the world, triumphed over death. This spirit has won! The old Law, whose body had been buried with Christ, has been clarified and resurrected in Spinoza. The kernel of a new covenant resides in the Master's teaching of salvation. Just as the ancients had a constitution of a holy state, so we shall receive a constitution of a holy empire [*Reichsverfassung*], because Christ has triumphed! . . .

(44)

All state constitutions which are not founded on the principle of the knowledge of God must collapse; because all fallacy must finally perish, and only truth endures eternally. Only where there is truth is there life; where it is suppressed, where lies rule, there is death. Even if divided and split, life may continue for a while, but God does not, however, constitute its essence.

History provides two great warning examples for our statement: we are shocked when we contemplate them as if they were nocturnal spectres, and turn our glance away. Both phenomena have long fallen into their graves; the one appears to us only as an ethereal fog – the other as a rigid cadaver - - - we mean the Jewish people, that spirit without body, and the Chinese, that body without spirit!

(45)

The cleavage which appeared in mankind after the downfall of the Jewish state will not endure for ever. Religion and politics will once again become one Whole, church and state will again permeate each other. Living knowledge will replace obsolete profession of faith; the one religion of the Spirit will replace the external, divided confessions. While in the past a blind belief based on authority was the pillar of society, now it will be enlightened science. Let us not complain about the grain of seed that it decomposes when it bears its fruit. Let us not say that because it has been created by God it must live for ever. Indeed, if what has lived once upon a time should live forever, then the Law of the Jews would have to have eternal force. He who lives believing in Christ, will also believe in the kingdom of truth.

(46)

True religion, the knowledge of God revealed in the holy history, is the only foundation of states, the basic law, out of which the other laws follow. Because the highest good of men is to be bound socially to all and not exclusively to one person – because nothing is more beneficial for man's achievement of his highest good than his brother – therefore men associate, create a great covenant, in order to support each other as brethren, as equal beings, in their pursuits. The less conscious men are of their highest good, the weaker, more transient, and less holy is their covenant; it becomes stronger, more enduring, and holier, the more conscious they become of their eternal salvation.

Our era, which has come to know God, will not enter into a covenant aimed at a terrestrial, transient goal: [it will do so] only for its highest salvation, the knowledge of God. Every holy constitution proceeds from the unity of consciousness of society, on which it then impacts by permeating it and thus ceases to act on it as an external law. It is then that the law has fulfilled its vocation, brings its cycle to a close, and the commonwealth in which it reigns rejuvenates itself, is being elevated to a higher life, which is detached from it in space and time. On the other hand, a constitution which does not proceed from the unity of consciousness of a society and out of the sum of its sciences and traditions, is not holy and misses it aim.

(47)

The history of mankind provides us with one living example of a constitution which did not fail to impress itself upon a people. Other nations have achieved more in certain pursuits, and have thus been of greater benefit to mankind. But out of all nations, this one has been the holy instrument through which the unity and essence of God has been revealed and did not therefore appear in external, defined forms. This nation relates to the many as man – the absolute form – relates to the organization of the earth with all its richness of forms.

We mean that ancient, holy nation-state [*Volksstaat*] which perished long ago, yet continues to live until this very day in the feelings of its scattered members. In the Jews, in this despised people that has remained loyal to its old customs and which, after a long slumber, awakens now once more to a higher consciousness and is just about to conclude its restless wandering, to which God had condemned it until it sees his countenance again; in the Jews, we say, their ancient Law is being revived again. This provides a more vivid testimony of its holiness than any other historical monument, more truthful than its holy books, more eloquent than all the salvaged documents of previous ages.

This nation has been summoned from the very beginning to conquer the world – not like pagan Rome by its force of arms, but through the inner virtue of its spirit. [The Jewish people] itself wandered like a ghost through the world it had conquered, and its enemies did not succeed in vanquishing it, because the spirit is intangible. This spirit has already permeated the world, and the world is yearning for a new constitution worthy of the Old Mother.

It will appear, this new holy constitution; the old Law will once again be resurrected in all its radiance. Out of the old world lost in chaos, the genius of mankind will rise as out of a deluge brought about by God. A Law shall appear which as the unity of mankind's consciousness will, in its turn, act upon mankind, permeate it, fulfil its calling, and conclude its cycle.

(48)

And in the later future, when this will come about, no new Law will appear; rather, mankind will be united-into-itself internally as well as externally: the Law of God will live in every member, and will be clearly recognized. Because external laws are necessary only so long as men feel the need to be enriched from the outside. But just as there has once been a time in which man – still a child – had no other needs than those satisfied by Nature, so there will come a time when man – now turned old – will have no other wishes than those which can be provided by his artistic activity [*Kunsttätigkeit*].

The end of the Holy History of Mankind

Socialism and Communism

[First published in *Einundzwanzig Bogen aus der Schweiz* (Twenty-One Sheets from Switzerland), ed. Georg Herwegh (Zurich and Winterthur, 1843).]

If it is true that our time still suffers from the contrast between theory and praxis, that the objective world, which the present has inherited from the past, is in conflict with the subjective world of our modern feelings and ideas – then this sickness is nowhere as dangerous, this contrast nowhere as sharp, as in Germany.

To what depth of sensitivity, to what clarity of consciousness, have the masters of German literature educated the spirit and disposition of their countrymen! In the heaven of our ideas no prejudice and no hate prevail: here, man's dignity is acknowledged to the fullest, his eternal rights proclaimed; here, all men are brothers and members of one family, here no institutions originating in the blind egoism of barbaric times exist and absolute equality rules supreme; how many sophisms are brought forward to reconcile the egoism which is incorporated in our external world with this absolute equality of men, how much pain is taken to paper over the chasm between what is essential in man and what is accidental in him, to confuse the normal with the abnormal, the true nature of man – spirit – with his still false, raw nature – all in order to reach the conclusion that there are as many human natures as there are different individuals. All this then points to the conclusion that in our deepest feelings we are, after all, convinced of the essential equality of all men. We discern this in our greatest poets, we recognize this in our most exalted thinkers.

Yes, Germany has travelled the furthest in theory – yet, alas, only in theory. The German is too spiritual, too universal, to focus on definite, concrete living conditions. He is so eminently impractical that he does not dare to attempt to introduce his ideas into living reality. He considers his most noble feelings, his most sublime thoughts, as beautiful dreams, as 'ideals'; and while other nations often surpass their own ideas through deeds – as, for example, the French in the first Revolution – the German nation, on the other hand, does not dare touch the hem of its feelings and thoughts with practical hands.

Thus while we are the freest of men, the purest democrats, the most radical communists, we suffer at the same time most gladly the inner strife [*Zerrissenheit*] of our actual life. We endure everything and look down from our exalted philosophical heights, even with religious resignation, on bad and corrupt reality. By not daring to introduce our ideas into life, we turn our eyes away from the present to the otherworldliness of the future. Nowhere did the religion of the otherworldly and the hereafter find a better soil than in Germany. Nowhere has the philosophy of the deed [*Philosophie der Tat*] to fight greater obstacles than with us, who still labour under the medieval world-sickness of the contrasts between theory and praxis, between politics and religion, between the here-and-now and the hereafter.

Yet it is only from Germany that the philosophy of the deed can draw its principles. It is only where philosophy has reached its culmination that it can transcend itself and proceed towards action. The contrast between thisworldliness and otherworldliness – engendered in the spirit and through the spirit – can be overcome only in the spirit and through the spirit.

In reality German philosophy has already forced its way towards the principle of the modern age and turned into the philosophy of the deed; yet we are still at the beginning of this important, spiritual process, [as] there are only a few who have the courage to turn the sharpness of their thought's sword towards the external world. Some abstract totally from life; others, who have come too near to reality to ignore it, try to come to terms with it as best they can – and since they are too weak to construct reality in accordance with their self-consciousness, they turn the weapon on themselves and try the suicidal attempt of shaping their own consciousness according to the bad reality.

To the latter belongs [Lorenz von] Stein's book *Der Socialismus und Communismus des heutigen Frankreichs – Ein Beitrag zur Zeitgeschichte* [The

Socialism and Communism of Present-Day France – A Contribution to Contemporary History],[1] in which he attempts to achieve an adequate judgment on the essence of a phenomenon which is gripping the modern world. We shall presently discuss his attempt more closely; but before we do that, we have to achieve a true judgment of this phenomenon as well as of its inner relationship to philosophy and modern spiritual life in general.

The last century has not yet advanced to the basic principle of the new age, though for the countries of culture [*Kulturstaaten*] of Europe it did pave the way for this principle – the absolute freedom of life – by developing the polemics and criticism against the medieval structure of social life based on state and church. Yet while it spread enlightenment about religion and politics, it left unchallenged the basis of these double phenomena, and limited itself to pointing out the 'abuses' which crept into church and state, caused (as it maintained) by the malice and stupidity of the leaders of these institutions; against these it recommended a 'rational' religion and a 'law-abiding' politics.

Just as the task of the last century was a double one and aimed at a double aim, one religious and one political, so there emerged also a division of labour of this task among two nations: the German nation applied itself primarily to the religious, the French mainly to the political area. Here it was Kant, there it was the Revolution that became the aim and the end of the previous century. From then on, there begins a new period in the history of the new age.

The former century wished to found a new state based on the rule of law [*Rechtsstaat*] and a new religion, the religion of reason. But it had barely succeeded in achieving its negative aim – the overthrow of the old politics and religion – when the inner contradiction of its further aims became apparent.

All politics – be it absolutist, aristocratic, or democratic – must, for the sake of its own preservation, maintain the contrast between domination

---

[1] Stein's book on French socialist and communist thinkers and movements was published in Leipzig in 1842. Stein was a Prussian official, with a philosophical Hegelian training, and his book was intended as a warning against the dangers of revolutionary movements; but because it was written mainly in a detached scholarly way, and included much information about French radical thought which was otherwise unavailable in Germany due to censorship, it became, paradoxically, a major source for German radicals about French socialist and communist literature. It is also in this context that Hess' article makes use of the information supplied in Stein's study.

and bondage; it has an interest in this contrast, since it owes its very existence to it. The same applies to the heavenly politics, to religion: not to this or that religion, but to religion as such, which is embedded in spiritual bondage: this contrast too cannot allow man to reach freedom of the spirit without negating itself, it too is interested that what is divine and ethical would appear to man as otherworldly and remain external, ensuring that he persists in the mere quest for these aims, since their attainment would make religion's own existence superfluous.

The previous century did indeed negate the old state, yet not the concept of the state as such, not the contrast among the conflicting, abstract personalities with their totally egoistic outcomes, i.e. not with the necessity of an external government or domination of these personalities. It was seeking to find the evil of the state, as of religion, not in the essence of these institutions, but in their accidental form or in the baseness or stupidity of state authorities or church leaders. And trying to found the 'state as based on the rule of law' or the 'religion of reason', one became quite frightened when finding out that there was not even one positive, organic idea behind all this sharp-witted and penetrating critique of understanding [*Verstand*].[2]

Religion was thus 'enlightened', but reason strove also against any new form of religion; the politics of the *ancien régime*, the old form of government, was overthrown, but no new 'Rechtsstaat' was successfully consolidated. Ever since Kant and the French Revolution a constant quest for a rational and just basis for state and church was futilely undertaken; it was futile for the simple reason that these medieval forms of social life are based neither on reason nor on justice but arise out of raw nature [*naturwüchsig*], out of the blind struggle of egoism and the needs of egoistic individuals.

In the meantime, while one was striving in public life for a new form for the overthrown medieval institutions and one form drove out another, without the latter offering more satisfaction than the former – all the while as this was going on, new and actually subversive ideas were developed quietly; these were not satisfied with dealing critically with the past, but were turned also in an organizing fashion towards the future. The basic principle of the new world was being discovered. In

---

[2] Hess follows here the Hegelian distinction between Reason (*Vernunft*) and Understanding (*Verstand*), the latter being a mere formal ratiocination, devoid of historical contextualization and hence of significance in the march of world history.

Germany, Fichte was the first to express, albeit in a somewhat raw and wild fashion, the autonomy of the spirit; with Baboeuf in France we see emerging the first, and hence equally raw, form of a unified social life. Put in a popular way: in Germany, from Fichte one dates the beginning of atheism, in France from Baboeuf the beginning of communism – or as Proudhon now expresses it more precisely – anarchy, i.e. the negation of all political domination, the negation of the concept of the state or politics.

Here the essentially new element, which has begun to develop with Fichte and Baboeuf in Germany and France has to be stressed. The commonly prevailing consciousness still clings to the achievements of the preceding century: thus in Germany, with few exceptions, everybody still thinks, consciously or unconsciously, within the Kantian categories of understanding, and 'religion within the boundaries of pure reason'[3] – i.e. that of abstract understanding – is still the great desired goal of the age; in France, on the other hand, nothing is more popular than the 'Rechtsstaat' with its 'popular representation', its 'equality before the law' and other such fictions. All the while, there develops quietly, on both banks of the Rhine – in Germany and in France – the principle of the future.

Kant is erroneously viewed as the founder of German philosophy, and an ingenious poet-philosopher, Heinrich Heine, has even drawn a parallel between the different phases of the French Revolution and those of German philosophy, putting next to each other as analogous phenomena Kant and Robespierre, Fichte and Napoleon, Schelling and the Restoration, Hegel and the July [1830] Revolution.[4]

But the true founder of German philosophy – if one wishes to name a personal representative for the spirit of the age [*Zeitgeist*] – is none other than [the thinker] whose world view lies equally at the foundation of French social philosophy – Spinoza; and as far as Heine's analogy goes, it is only Kant and Robespierre, i.e. the religious revolution, who are analogous phenomena. German philosophy, on the other hand – this positive development of the freedom of the spirit which began with Fichte and ended with Hegel – has so little in common in principle with the further experiments of French politics, that one needs indeed the fantasy of a poet to find any analogies here.

---

[3] The reference is to Kant's 1793 essay of that name.
[4] Hess alludes here to Heinrich Heine's work *History of Religion and Philosophy in Germany*, already mentioned by him in *The Holy History of Mankind* (see above, n. 6 to *The Holy History of Mankind*, p. 40).

Yet German philosophy, which up to Hegel has been merely an esoteric science [*Wissenschaft*],⁵ and only now, as speculative atheism, begins to have its impact on actual life, is much more analogous, even identical, with French social philosophy which also begins now, after St. Simon and Fourier, to emancipate itself from scholasticism and to penetrate into the people as scientific communism [*wissenschaftlicher Kommunismus*]. The similarity between these two phenomena is not poetical, but can be proved philosophically.

After Baboeuf's communism and Fichte's idealism drove themselves into the ground through their own nihilism, we see in Germany the emergence of Schelling and Hegel and in France that of St Simon and Fourier. The principle of the new age – the absolute unity of all life – which manifested itself in Germany as abstract idealism and in France as abstract communism, begins now to develop out of itself its own concrete content.

As men of feeling, Schelling and St Simon reached their results through unmediated intuition [*Anschauung*] and, without first spiritualizing them through the dialectic of speculation, then presented these to an astonished world which is moved more through persuasion than conviction. This is not yet the true result, because it has not been achieved through scientific means.

The principle of the new age does, however, achieve a firm footing in various areas which it touches in Germany and France: it becomes a power, and before its life-giving breath the dead and rigid contradictions of the bad reality disappear – here in social life, there in nature. But this power has not yet achieved its justification, it has not yet legitimized itself before the spirit; due to its immediacy, it tears at men's hearts and finds acceptance among the young, who are more receptive to all that is good and great than to the strictly scientifically constructed teachings of Hegel and Fourier which appear simultaneously; but ultimately it will have to vacate the field to the higher power of science.

If one views the writings of those authors who apparently work in different fields and stand in no external relationship to each other, and then compares the fate of their theories, one would be astounded by their similarity. With Hegel and Fourier this similarity goes as far as

---

⁵ See above, n. 8 to *The Holy History of Mankind* (p. 42), for Hess' usage of the term *Wissenschaft*, as referring to the whole realm of knowledge, not merely to the natural sciences. It is in this sense that Hess refers later to *wissenschaftlicher Kommunismus* – i.e. communism based on knowledge and social analysis, not on mere moralistic wishful thinking – a term which would later find its way into Marx's thought.

the construction of new words and sentence structures. In the case of St Simon, who unlike his German spiritual brother, Schelling, did not survive himself,[6] one can maintain that if he would still vegetate today, he – like Schelling – would have joined the conservatives, as has been the case with his eminent disciples, e.g. Michel Chevalier.

It is essentially the same task which both the German and the French spirit have taken upon themselves. And if someone still has a doubt about the unifying basic principle out of which in Germany there emerged the teaching of the absolute freedom of the spirit and in France that of absolute social equality with all its consequences – he should go one step further than these theories and should follow their practical outcome as they manifest themselves now and specially here, on the frontier between Germany and France; were he to do so, the last doubt about the equal tendencies in Germany and France would vanish like fog before the sun.

In so far as they begin to have an impact on actual life, French social theories are today getting closer to Baboeuf's communism; but in their essence they go much beyond him, just as today's German philosophy, which is linked by its energy and passion for action to Fichte's atheism, yet goes similarly beyond it. Between Baboeuf and contemporary communism there lies the whole fullness of French social philosophy, just as between Fichte and contemporary atheism there lies the whole dialectic of German philosophy.

The great idea of Fourier, who based the organization of labour on the fullest freedom of the movement of all inclinations, is not lost to contemporary communism; and despite the fact that all concessions which Fourier, like Hegel, makes to existing reality, thus deforming their systems aesthetically, morally, and intellectually and which make a closer association with Fourier and Hegel impossible – yet it is precisely in communism, under the conditions of community [*Gemeinschaft*], that Fourier's main idea achieves its true meaning and practical application, just as the Hegelian idea of the 'absolute personality' achieves only in atheism its true meaning and is saved from misinterpretations.

Through Fourier and Hegel the French and German spirit have thus been elevated to the absolute point of view on which is based the infinite justification of the subject, i.e. personal freedom or the absolutely free

---

[6] This unkind reference to Schelling's longevity is a jibe at his later philosophy, which tended to be politically extremely conservative and theologically semi-mystical if not obscurantist, as against his earlier contributions to the radical innovations of German philosophical idealism.

personality, as well as the law of the not less justified objective world, the absolute equality of all persons in society: and these two are no longer contrasts, but are the mutually complementing moments of one and the same principle – the principle of the absolute freedom of all life.

A very popular objection is being raised against communism, namely that the condition of community, in which the absolute freedom of all men and all activity reigns supreme, without an external law or a government of any sort defending this freedom against arbitrariness – that such a social condition is an 'ideal' one and presupposes not men but 'angels': this quite justified objection is being overcome here. Fourier and Hegel have recognized that there exists only one human nature, just as there exists only one principle of life and not a good and a bad one, neither angels and devils, nor virtuous and lascivious men. And as Fourier approached social conditions with this higher view of life and applied it to them, he discovered that *every* inclination is good when it is not frustrated through external obstacles or, conversely, is not being morbidly excited through reaction to it, but is freely welcome and can carry out its activity.

This is the secret which Spinoza has already expressed in his *Ethics*, which has however achieved its meaning for the objective world of human society only through Fourier, just as it has achieved its true meaning for the subjective world of the human spirit through Hegel. Fourier solved the problem of social equality and was able to remove the popular-reasonable objection that it presupposes the absolute equality of 'angels', by explicitly rejecting the negation of property – and has thus done the greatest service to communism; in the same way Hegel had solved the problem of personal freedom and thus – equally without intending it – removed another objection. The German spirit – not yet fully developed – militated against a society in which all personal property and (so it is assumed) all personal freedom would be destroyed. But through Hegel the German spirit reached the realization that the freedom of the person should not be sought in the uniqueness of the individual but in what is common to all human beings. Every concept which is not a common human property, which is not universal to all, cannot promote my freedom – yea, only this is truly my inalienable property which is at the same time also a common good.

A particular, individual property is being stolen from me when it is at the same time stolen from all others. Proudhon had hit the nail on the head when he answered the question *qu'est que c'est la propriété?* by *la propriété c'est le vol.*[7] Thus the French and the German spirit have made the basic principle of the new age into truth.

But in order to actualize this truth in life itself, those two moments – personal freedom and social equality – have to be reunited. Without absolute equality, without French communism on the one side, and without absolute freedom, without German atheism on the other, neither personal freedom nor social equality can become an actual, realized truth. So long as the state of conflict and dependence finds recognition in the objective world, so long as politics rules the world, liberation from heavenly politics is unthinkable. Religion and politics stand and fall together, because the inner unfreedom of the spirit – heavenly politics – supports external subjection, and vice versa. Just as in communism, in the condition of community, no religion is conceivable, because it – the principle of alienation and unfreedom – necessarily pushes towards the negation of communism – so, on the other hand, no politics is conceivable under atheism, the condition of spiritual freedom. When Robespierre wished to replace the old fallen compact politics by the phantom of a 'free politics', he had first of all to decree that the Convention recognize the existence of a 'Supreme Being'– i.e. he could not bring to life the phantom of a state based on the rule of law [*Rechtsstaat*], without the phantom of a 'Religion of Reason'.

After having established the essence of French communism in its inner relationship to German atheism on the one hand and to the modern world on the other, let us move now to Stein's description of this phenomenon and see what he makes of it!

Stein did feel that socialism and communism differ in that the one is more a theory, while the other gets involved directly in practical life, that socialism focuses mainly on the organization of labour, while communism encompasses the whole of human life and within it a radical reform – the abolition [*Aufhebung*] of private property – is dominant. Yet we say that despite this difference in the results of socialism and communism, he felt that the basic principle of both is identical. This is so partly because of their historical simultaneous emergence and development, partly because of their unmistakable inner relationship to each other – since both direct their main attempt at the proletariat – have made it necessary for Stein to look for a common basis for both phenomena.

---

[7] The reference is to Proudhon's famous battle-cry: 'What is property? Property is theft.'

This basis he has found in the democratic spirit, which became apparent in France before the Revolution, came into life with it, and during and after it developed further even more strongly. Another person might perhaps have maintained that Liberty, rather than Equality, is the principle of the current French spiritual direction, and by following this fallacy would have totally lost sight of what makes France unique in the current movement of the time, especially as compared to Germany. It is quite true: it is Equality which is the specific element of modern France, and it was not an accident that Philippe of Orleans adopted the name *Egalité*. But that this basis alone is not sufficient in explaining the phenomena of social life in contemporary France; that ultimately it is not a principle, but is itself a moment of the great principle which moves the modern world (even if, as we have admitted, this specific moment prevails currently mainly in France); that at that same time French social developments since the Revolution do not have a sufficient foundation in it – all this should have shed a light on the essence of Equality itself, which is unthinkable without Liberty and Unity; yet it would also have thrown a light on the revolutionary history, which did indeed have *Egalité* at the centre and focus of its forefront, yet never forgot next to it Liberty and Unity. In revolutionary history, *Liberté, Egalité,* and *Unité* always form the Holy Trinity which inflamed the hearts in the fight against oppression, injustice, and lies of all sorts.

Yet Stein closed his eyes to this [phenomenon] and refused to recognize it, because he did not relate to this whole development of our time in a knowledgeable way. Yet we have to admit that it is nothing but a fortunate instinct that Stein emphasizes so much *Egalité*: he felt oppressed by the democratic movement in whose midst he wrote his book – he breathed its air, and this air squeezed worried groans out of his chest. Yes, Stein foresees the gathering storm that will shatter the foundations of society – not because he knows the spiritual elements, but because, like an animal, he lives with its material elements and has come in immediate contact with them; thus the future does not enlighten him, it only frightens him. The 'principle' of which he speaks has for him no solid ground: as he said, he has snatched it from the air, more precisely from the air which in France is pregnant with the elements of equality.

The true principle of the direction of the French spirit lies deeper. Truth, which manifests itself on the one hand as subjective freedom, on the other as objective equality or justice – truth whose essential feature is unity – is, strictly speaking, the principle of the modern French, as well as German, spiritual movement. The good Stein has totally misunderstood this whole principle; hence the French spiritual movement appeared to him as one-sided. It is indeed one-sided, it followed one specific aspect of truth, the aspect of justice, because it is dedicated more to action than to the [mere] idea. But this movement is therefore in no way a mistake or fallacy. It has an explicitly decisive relation to its opposite; it is conscious of this relation, as it does not lack the mediating element – truth or the principle of unity. According to Stein's description, *Egalité* truly floats in the air: one does not know whence it has come, hence one cannot know whither it goes. But how can France be responsible for the fact that a German 'Doctor of Law' cannot achieve an understanding of what moves the French spirit? The whole of Stein's book is basically nothing else than a long groan, which is what one can expect from those who cannot grasp the positive substance of our modern strivings and therefore imagine that they can nonetheless stand above them – and who then bemoan the 'negative' tendencies of the age because they are incapable of perceiving their positive content.

The crude mistake to which Stein is then driven, due to his skewed perception of the French spirit, is that he perceives in the striving for equality only an external, material aspect aimed at mere pleasure. While he himself excuses the so-called materialism of our age by seeing it merely as the first attempt of the abstract personality to gain for itself a concrete content, he finds in communism only the striving of the proletariat to achieve for itself the same pleasures as those of the property owners.

It is however one of the major achievements of communism that in it the contrast between pleasure and work disappears. Only under the conditions of alienated property is pleasure divorced from work. The condition of community [*Gemeinschaft*] is the practical actualization of that philosophical ethics, which recognizes in free activity the true and only pleasure, the so-called highest good. By contrast, the condition of alienated property is the practical actualization of egoism and immorality, which on one hand negates free activity and on the other replaces the highest good of man with animal-like pleasure as if it were the noble aim of an equally animal-like labour. Stein is still stuck in the midst of these abstractions of labour and pleasure, while communism has long ago moved beyond it and has already become – admittedly first in the mind of its initial representatives – what it should become in reality: p r a c t i c a l   e t h i c s.

Stein knows communism only in its first, most crude form: what has happened to the idea of communism since Baboeuf – the teachings of

St Simon, Fourier, Proudhon, and so on – he sees not as stages of development and transition of that idea, but isolates them as independent phenomena of whose connection with the general idea of *Egalité* he does have an inkling, but whose special impact on communism he has not grasped at all; hence he groups Proudhon next to Lamennais and because he does not know where to place him, he makes him into a 'marginal writer'! Proudhon is for him not a communist, despite the fact that he criticizes and negates personal or private property in the sharpest way. Obviously, according to the picture which he, Stein, paints of Proudhon, Proudhon cannot be a communist – since Proudhon is scientific! But neither can he be in Stein's sense a socialist, since he negates private property; ergo he is a 'marginal writer'!

Stein totally dissociates socialism proper from communism; he presents a meagre abstraction of the theories of St Simon and Fourier, which can be found in already published German translations and in separate accounts which are as good as his; but there is no inkling of the essential link between their theories and those of communism. He imagined being able to take care of everything with his pitiful category of *Egalité*. Besides this, his book is a thoughtless compilation, a throwing together of St Simon, Fourier, Leroux, Lamennais, Proudhon, Baboeuf, Cabet, and so on, who are trooped out in a certain order, row after row, man next to man, like Prussian toy soldiers.

After his introduction, Stein should have started his account with Baboeuf. The first form of communism emerged directly out of Sansculottism.[8] The kind of equality which Baboeuf had in mind was therefore the equality of the Sansculottes, the equality of poverty. Wealth, luxury, the arts and sciences were to be abolished, the cities destroyed – Rousseau's state of nature was the phantom which spooked around in people's heads. The wide field of industry was still a *terra incognita* for this kind of communism. It was the most abstract communism, equality was to be achieved in a negative way, by killing every kind of desire. It was a monkish, Christian communism – but without any hereafter, without any hope for a better future. Only natural necessities were acknowledged as real, and even this only on the basis of utter need. Could men have been created without bodies, then the body would also have been negated. Since this was not possible, agriculture was left as the means of satisfying bodily needs. This poorest form of communism

---

[8] The so-called 'shirtless' of the French Revolution in its radical, Jacobin stage.

could not develop its theory, since it itself negated all science; it had therefore to become practical at once. But reality was already on a higher stage than this state of nature; hence [this communism] soon faltered.[9]

[On the other hand,] Stein recounts clearly and in a straightforward way the causes which under the [Napoleonic] Empire and the Restoration hindered externally the development of the democratic spirit, while furthering within society the contrast between bourgeoisie and proletariat: out of this there emerged the spirit which could appear in its manifold richness after the July Revolution.

There are, however, many repetitions in the book: thus, for example, the connection between communism and the proletariat is repeated ad nauseam. This is the only lively side which Stein would like to take away from communism. Regarding the justification for the demands of the proletariat, he glides over them nicely with a few philosophical empty phrases, and his lack of insight proves his inability to grasp the issue. He could have achieved such an understanding only through a realization of the connection of communism with socialism and science – an insight which, as already stated, he totally lacks.

How Stein actually imagines the solution of the social problems (whose importance he recognizes) – the final reconciliation of the proletariat and the bourgeoisie, or the tensions between the aristocracy of money and pauperism – this cannot be learned with certainty from his book, though here and there some arguments are bandied about. That much is certain: in communism, which he does not understand, he sees only a bogeyman, but not a reconciliation. He must therefore seek a reconciliation of the antagonisms in the existing conflictual situation. This he also silently admits by some quiet phrases, and thus – as well as through his polemic against the 'negative' tendencies in Germany – secures for himself a place among the 'mediators'.

---

[9] It is interesting to compare this to Marx's description of 'crude communism' in his *Economic-Philosophical Manuscripts* which were written a year later (1844): 'This crude communism . . . wishes to eliminate talent, etc., by force . . . [This is] shown by the abstract negation of the whole world of culture and civilization, and the regression to the unnatural simplicity of the poor and wantless individual who has not only not surpassed private property but has not yet even attained it.' See Karl Marx, *Early Writings*, trans. T. B. Bottomore (London, 1963), pp. 153–4. The same criticism of early theories of communism reappears again in *The Communist Manifesto*, where Marx claims that they 'inculcated universal asceticism and social levelling in its crudest forms'. See Karl Marx and Friedrich Engels, *Selected Works* (Moscow, 1962), I, p. 61.

But in reality, a mediation of the contradictions in the situation of strife is unthinkable. Stein brings up the trivial statement that, since the old distinctions among the [medieval] estates have disappeared, now everyone can acquire property; yet, on the other hand, he realizes that this 'right' of acquisition is only an illusion, since where acquired or inherited property is connected with the 'right' of the abstract personality, with talent and work, it necessarily prevails over mere 'right', over talent which is impecunious and does not control any means. It appears as if Stein finds a way out of this dilemma in the abolition of the inheritance of property, though he never says so explicitly. But here, as anywhere else, there is no mediation between two contradictory principles.

The principle of private property means that everyone can dispose of his property freely according to his will: I can bequeath or give away my property, otherwise it is not *my* property; usually I will leave it to my children or my next of kin or even my friends – but not to the state, not to the commonwealth. Should inheritance be abolished, as the St Simonists wish, then private property as such would be abolished, and what is then left is only to understand the meaning and essence of communism. As we have seen, Baboeuf does not grasp this; neither did St Simon – he has only order on his mind, not liberty. He wanted a hierarchy – the worst of all forms of government, because it is the most consistent one. But where liberty is destroyed, neither equality, nor justice can exist.

St Simon wanted Equality without Liberty, Fourier, on the other hand, wanted Liberty without Equality: just as the one was keen on innovations and in his practical zeal neglected theory, so the latter was too conservative, and wanted to reconcile a totally new and truly original idea – that of absolutely free labour – with existing reality.

The latest social reformers and communists have, however, arrived at a point of grasping the concept of communism in all its sharpness and depth. Only through absolute liberty – not only of 'labour' in the old, constricted sense, but of every and all human inclination and activity – is the absolute equality, or rather community, of all conceivable 'goods' also possible; and conversely, it is only in such a community that liberty is thinkable.

Labour – society itself – should not be organized, but organizes itself by itself inasmuch as everyone does what he cannot avoid, and avoids what he cannot do. Every man delights in some activity, even in many-sided activities; and out of the multiplicity of free human inclinations or activities emerges the free, not dead and stilted, but living, ever-young organism of free human society, of free human occupations, which now ceases to be 'labour' and becomes totally identical with 'pleasure'.

No more can there be talk of a 'mediation' between communism and the principle of personal property. From here onwards, the true, conscious battle of principles begins. Previous history has not fully realized the principle of personal property; the nearer we come to the modern age, the more we find this principle making concessions to its opposite, communism. Previous history has been only a blind, raw battle between the abstract universal – the state – and the egoism of the individual, civil society [*bürgerliche Gesellschaft*]. Only in civil society does the principle of personal property dominate in its purity. But through the principle of abstract personal freedom, the right of property has turned into its opposite: the personal right of property brought about slavery.

The effort of millennia was needed to achieve the victory of the state based on the abstract rule of law. It too had to turn into its opposite, because it had civil society as its opposing enemy. Universal right turns, under conditions of friction, strife, and egoism, into universal injustice. When it reaches its apex, the state based on the rule of law is either the right of the individual who concentrates the state in himself and says of himself *l'état c'est moi*[10] – or it is popular sovereignty. But not only in these two formulas, but also in the hybrid [form] of the 'constitutional monarchy', in the middle ground between monarchy and republic, has the abstract state based on the rule of law been negated historically through its own dialectics.

Let us take only one example, that of the republic, since this is the darling of many German philosophers. Here the state based on the rule of law is supposed to endow the people with sovereignty; but since it is called to guarantee abstract personal liberty – i.e. personal property – it must, as the abstract unity or universality of the various personalities, place itself above and against them. A contradiction is thus emerging, as the people, which should rule itself, is split into the ruling and the ruled, mastery and bondage. The right to legislate, which should belong to the whole people, is necessarily practised only by a part of it – namely by that part of the people which succeeds, either through force or cunning, to grab power for itself. The courtiers and government lackeys are therefore right when they say that the form of government in a state does not matter.

---

[10] 'I am the state' – the notorious statement attributed to King Louis XIV of France.

The positive state based on the rule of law, as it has existed in North America since the latter half of the last century and in Europe partly since the French Revolution, is admittedly an improvement on the feudalistic, theocratic, and despotic forms, i.e. on states still in thrall to the raw forms of property, descent, nationality, religion, and so on; yet the state based on the rule of law, which has itself not yet overcome the raw, natural determinations [*Naturbestimmtheiten*] but only sidelined them, is closer to these human societies than to the absolute human society, i.e. communism. This is, just as Protestantism is, an advance over Catholicism, yet is still closer to it than to atheism. Had I had the choice between North America and Russia, or between French and Austrian politics, I would still choose the first, just as I would prefer the Protestant to the Catholic religion. But as a matter of principle, the form of government is irrelevant – each and all of them are in their essence the opposite of absolute freedom and equality – from despotism to the republic, from the hereditary monarchy, which emerges directly from civil society, to representative government based on majority voting, which has overcome the natural element of personal property in the *form* of the state: all of them still harbour mastery and bondage. In the best case, it is the minority which is dominated by the majority.

The representative system, which has become a necessity in our larger states, makes it necessary at the same time that even under a radical election law, the rule of the majority is an illusion: it necessarily turns into the rule of a minority, as only a minority can rule. But even it possesses only illusory power, since once the people feel its power, once it becomes a real power, it is being brought down. This game will be repeated until the state – the condition of conflict and strife – destroys itself dialectically and makes room for the one and united form of social life – that of a community.

We still have to look forward to a work that will describe the historical development of communism. In this respect, Stein's book leaves not much, but everything, to be desired.

Finally, we would like to discuss the relationship of Stein, a Hegelian of the middle, to communism. Stein is a political realist: hence he is incapable of a clear judgment not only of political atheism, i.e. communism, but also of the positive state based on the rule of law, above which he stands only apparently; at every moment he is prone to fall victim to accidents and reactionary tendencies, because he chases the *phantom* of a state based on the rule of law, 'the rational state' [*Vernunftstaat*], which exists only in the mind of political rationalists, just as the 'religion of reason' [*Vernunftreligion*] is only a fiction of religious rationalists.

For this is the case: Hegel wished to conceive the state as actual reason [*wirkliche Vernunft*].[11] He therefore encompassed [in his writings] not only the sphere of law, but the totality of human life. In this view the concept 'state' becomes coeval with that of the absolute human society. But absolute human society cannot be thought of as being fixed in place and time; the life of human society is the life of world history. But in world history, the state is being overcome and abolished [*aufgehoben*].[12] What happened to Hegel with religion, happened to him as well with the state, because he attributed the 'Absolute' to both; by trying to endow them with an 'eternal' foundation, he abolished both of them.

Stein belongs to those Hegelians who have 'misunderstood' their teacher and who still dream of an 'absolute', 'rational' state (as well as of a 'rational, absolute' religion); they get involved in fallacies and provide their opponents with a weapon. These Hegelians, with their 'rational state', have become a laughing stock, and one could actually ridicule them and destroy this with the same justification with which Bruno Bauer ridicules, from the point of view of religion, 'the strong ass Issachar'.[13] Those who are political rationalists and not yet political atheists direct their critique not at the state as such, but at this or that state, at this or that form of government; and while the phantom of a 'rational state' or 'religion of reason' still spooks in their head, they actually presuppose the dependence of man at the same moment as they presume his independence and his freedom.

---

[11] Here too Hess follows closely Hegel's philosophy by using the term *wirklich* (literally: actual, from *wirken*, to act) to suggest the active, not merely contemplative, aspect of Reason as acting-in-the-world.

[12] The Hegelian term *Aufhebung* meaning abolition, overcoming, and raising to a higher level all at the same time, is a key concept in his dialectics which sees development as occurring by constant internal changes which by realizing a principle – or a stage of development – also transcend it and overcome it.

[13] The reference is to the Left Hegelian Bruno Bauer who in his anonymous tract *Die Posaune des jüngsten Gerichts über Hegel den Atheisten und Anti-Christen: Ein Ultimatum* (The Trumpet of the Day of Judgment against Hegel the Atheist and Anti-Christ: An Ultimatum) (Leipzig, 1841), sharply criticized a literal reading of the Bible. The specific instance alluded to here by Hess is the characterization of Issachar, one of the sons of Jacob, as 'a strong ass' in Genesis 49:14; this was used by Bauer as an extreme example of how only a metaphorical reading of the biblical text makes sense.

Their liberalism [*Liberalität*] is a fiction – they are liberal only in one sphere, which is not actual and cannot have actuality. The 'rational state' is either not a state, or it is not the actuality of reason, since the latter negates the determinations of property, religion, nationality, government – in short: the whole content of the state, without which it would be superfluous. [This sphere] acknowledges only the absolute freedom of man – a freedom which can be realized only in an absolute human society, not in this or that one, which is still afflicted with raw natural determinations. But since the rationalist politicians posit such a human society, such a state, as absolute, they arrive only at the actuality of *reason*: whenever they descend to the actuality of *life*, they become reactionary. In this actuality of reason, there does not yet exist in praxis a human society which corresponds to their concept. All that exist are only states, i.e. societies, which are still afflicted with those raw natural determinations mentioned earlier. As such, they are not called upon to actualize absolute freedom, but only that degree of freedom, that degree of rationality, which accords with *their* point of view.

There obviously exist higher and lower forms of state and government. For example, the caste system, or the system of estates, has been presently overcome; we have actual states which have at least overcome raw natural determinations as states, even if they have not done so as human societies; we have actual states which move purely in the sphere of law – and everything else which falls beyond it, e.g. religion, descent and ancestry, personal property, i.e. private law – has not been overcome, but has been – as said before – sidelined. This means it has been separated from the state as not belonging to it; thus we have actual states which proclaim, for example, the separation of state and church.

The most advanced modern states hail this basic principle; there are others in which these more free principles have not been introduced, where they are not yet actual, positive, but where they are possible, because the consciousness of the people has already accepted these more liberal principles.

The rationalist politicians do not want to hear of these more liberal principles: they want their 'rational state', and since this is a fiction, in reality they do not want liberal principles. Hence it should not surprise us that one of these Hegelian (political) rationalists maintains that Protestants, Catholics, and Jews do not have a right to be treated equally in the state, since they cannot be 'rational' citizens so long as they are not [just] human beings, i.e. atheists and not any more Protestants [Catholics,

Jews] etc.. [14] Nor should one wonder that those who advocate 'freedom of teaching' do not really take this seriously and do not support the principle of the separation of school and state.

One should not be surprised by these and similar reactionary attitudes, since the political rationalists do not know how to give its due to the positive state based on the rule of law or to absolute human society. They are liberal neither in theory nor in praxis, only on the level of their fictional 'rational state'. Stein belongs to the middle Hegelians also regarding religion, and we should not wonder that he understands neither the positive [aspects] of contemporary conditions, nor the theoretical truth of communism and sees and bemoans everywhere only pure 'negation' and 'destructive tendencies'.

[14] This refers to the views of Bruno Bauer, expressed in his essay *Die Fähigkeit der heutigen Juden und Christen, frei zu sein* (The Ability of Contemporary Jews and Christians to be Free), published in the same collection of *Einundzwanzig Bogen aus der Schweiz*, in which Hess' own article appeared. Bauer's view that both Christians and Jews have first of all to give up their respective religious beliefs before they can truly become citizens, was also criticized in great detail at the same time in Karl Marx's *On The Jewish Question*, in which he argued that Bauer totally misses the distinction between merely political emancipation (i.e. equality before the law) and ultimate human, social emancipation, and thus arrives at an intolerant and oppressive formula.

A Communist *Credo*: Questions and Answers

[First published as an anonymous brochure in 1844, later reprinted in *Rheinische Jahrbücher zur Gesellschaftlichen Reform* (Rhenish Yearbooks for Social Reform), Darmstadt: Constanz, 1846.]

I. Of Labour and Enjoyment

1. What is the meaning of working?
Every transformation of matter for the life of mankind means working – or acting, creating, generating, manufacturing, producing, taking action and dealing, being active, in short: living. Because truly, all that lives, works; and regarding human life, not only through the head and hands, but also through all other limbs and organs of the human body which transform for human life the materials which they receive from outside, e.g. the mouth processes the received materials for the stomach, and the latter does the same for the blood and so on. This means that each organ of the human body, like each member of society, produces for the whole or works and creates even while it appears to be merely consuming and enjoying; at the same time it only enjoys its own life when it appears to work or produce for the whole. This harmony of work and pleasure takes place only in organic or organized life, not in the un-organized one, as we shall presently show.

2. What kinds of work exist?
Organized and unorganized. In other words: free and coerced or forced labour.

3. What is free activity and what is forced labour?

Free activity is all that grows out of an inner drive; forced labour, on the other hand, is all that happens out of external drive or out of need. If labour takes place out of an inner drive, it is a passion which promotes the enjoyment of life, a virtue which carries its own reward in itself. If, on the other hand, it is brought about through an external drive, then it becomes a burden which degrades human nature and oppresses it, a vice which can be carried out only for the vile wages of sin: it is wage or slave labour. A man who looks for the wages of his work outside himself is a slave who acts for alien goals, a mere machine driven [by others].

4. Which of these kinds of labour is understood today under work?
Forced labour.

5. What does one actually call free activity?
It is called either pleasure or virtue.

6. What does one understand today by pleasure?
Living according to certain sensual inclinations, without regard for the whole of human nature.

7. What does one understand today by virtue?
Living according to certain spiritual inclinations, without regard for the whole of human nature.

8. Can we nowadays act according to our true human nature or truly enjoy our human life?

Absolutely not. Almost every activity in our society comes not from an inner drive of our human nature, not out of passion and love of labour, but out of external pressure, usually because of need or money. On the other hand, those life activities which are caused by inner drives, which we call pleasure or virtue, are perverted in such a way that they hurt the living enjoyment of human nature even more than this occurs through coercive labour. The excesses in the satisfaction of certain sensual and spiritual life activities, which do not correspond to human nature and to which man now feels drawn only because his nature is not yet fully developed but is being oppressed – such excesses cause all free-living activity of contemporary man to assume an inhuman or bestial character. Thus drinking turns into boozing, the act of procreation or sexual love into unbridled lasciviousness, taking a rest from strenuous work into laziness, scholarship into pedantry, the striving of the heart after a higher life into hypocritical piety, virtue into self-torture, and so on. All sensual as well as spiritual inclinations deteriorate into excesses and become diseased because not all of human nature is developed but is rather oppressed and therefore degenerates. This disease then replaces all other inclinations of human nature and degrades man to the level of a beast which possesses only one-sided urges.

9. Is it possible for all human beings to live and enjoy [life] according to their nature?
Not only is this possible, but the opposite would have been impossible had human nature developed in all men and not been violently oppressed through social conditions.

10. What kinds of work are possible in a society in which human nature is developed in all men and in which every man can apply all his faculties?
In such a society nothing but free activity is possible.

11. What kinds of work are possible in a society in which men are neither fully developed, nor can human faculties be fully applied?
In such a society nothing is possible except coercive labour, sloth, seeking of pleasure, and false virtue.

12. Can, in our contemporary society, all human faculties be developed and the developed faculties applied?
No way. We are stunted both in our development as well as in the application of our faculties and powers. General education and human development [*Bildung*], as well as the exchange and application of our faculties, are impossible in our society. Most human powers remain undeveloped and those which are developed are being regularly crushed. The life of men in contemporary society is, in most cases, divided into coercive labour, deprivation, and the seeking of pleasure. Here one splashes in luxury, there one lives in famine; sometimes it is scarcity, sometimes it is surplus which degrades man to the level of a beast.

13. Why is the development and application of our human powers not possible in contemporary society?
Because we turn each other into slaves by buying and selling ourselves, or – what is the same – all our human powers.

II. Of Money and Mastery

14. What is money?
It is human activity expressed in numbers, the buying price or exchange value of our life.

15. Can human activity be measured in numbers?
Human activity can be as little paid for as human life itself. Because human activity *is* human life, and this cannot be weighed in any sum of money; it is immeasurable and invaluable [*unschätzbar*].

16. What is he who can be sold for money or sells himself for money?
He who can be sold for money is a slave, and he who sells himself has the soul of a slave.

17. What should we conclude from the existence of money?
We have to conclude that the consequence of the existence of money is slavery, as it is itself the sign of human bondage, because it is human worth expressed in numbers.

18. How much longer will men remain slaves and sell themselves, with all their powers, for money?
They will do so until every man is offered and guaranteed by society the means necessary to live and act in a human way, so that the individual will no longer need to procure these means on his own and have to sell his activity for this purpose in order to buy other men's activity. This human traffic, this spiritual exploitation, this so-called private enterprise, cannot be overcome merely by a decree: it can only be abolished by the creation of a communist society, in which everyone will be offered the means for the development and application of his capacities.

19. Is the existence of money in a communist society possible or imaginable?
Just as little as the existence of human slavery. Once men no longer need to exploit each other and haggle over their faculties and capacities, then they will not need any more to measure their worth in numbers: no longer will they need to count and pay [*zählen und bezahlen*]. In place of human worth measured in figures the true, immeasurable value of man will appear; instead of the increase of usury, human faculties and living pleasure will grow; instead of an hostile battle of rivalry, fought with dishonest weapons, harmonious cooperation and noble competition; instead

of multiplication tables, the head and heart and hands of free, active human beings.

III. Of Wealth and Freedom

20. What is wealth?
We call wealth the fruits of nature and the products of labour which serve as means for human life and human activity.

21. Can an individual create wealth without the cooperation of his fellow-men or the forces of nature?
No. Individual man, with all his powers, faculties, and means, is only a product of nature and human society; as a solitary individual he is powerless, and as such cannot produce wealth. Man can live and act only in connection with nature and humanity.

22. Who, then, produces wealth?
Nature and human society.

23. Are the fruits of nature the property of any single individual?
No, they are the common property of the commonalty of men.

24. Are the products of human society the property of any single individual?
No, they are the property of society.

25. What is he who collects and accumulates for himself alone the products of society and the fruits of nature?
He is a robber; he takes away from society what belongs to it and over which it should have dominion in the interests of all. He is a murderer: by robbing his neighbour of the means without which he cannot live and act, he robs him at the same time of his life or freedom.

26. How do we call, and what do we today consider, such a murderous robber who takes away from his fellow-man the fruits of [his] labour?
We hold him to be a rich gentleman, a wealthy man, property holder or owner.

27. What is in a communist society the property of an individual?
The guaranteed possession of what he needs for his life and activity.

28. Does our contemporary society guarantee the individuals what they need for their life and activity?

Only that possession is guaranteed to them which they acquire externally under certain legally defined forms and which they take away from each other by chance through inheritance, usury, gambling, the stock exchange, haggling [*Schacher*] and legal fraud.

29. Do individuals come through such acquisitions into the possession of what they need for their life and activity?

The answer to this is given by the misery, ignorance, and sinking into bestiality of those who carouse in idleness and of those who acquire, defraud, and engage in slave-labour.

30. Does then our society guarantee to each his own?

No way.

31. Can one then speak of civil [*bürgerliche*] freedom without guaranteed [*verbürgtes*] property?

Without guaranteed property only arbitrariness and despotism hold sway.

32. What is freedom?

A being is free when he does not need to coerce his nature in any way, but can live and act according to his nature and express his essence unhindered.

33. Can man live and act according to his nature in our society?

He has constantly to violate his nature. Never can he satisfy his thirst for knowledge, his artistic urge, his mechanical skills, his appetite – yea, even his hunger and thirst and his primary bodily needs of life.

34. How does one guarantee people's freedom and their true property or wealth?

This happens primarily through education.

35. What is understood by education?

First of all, bodily development, which is the foundation for any further development: it begins in the mother's womb. Secondly, the general human education in public institutions, where the seeds are sown and taken care of for any human virtue and faculty. From these institutions pupils graduate and are introduced to those fields of activity for which they possess the greatest inclination and the best talents. Here human social education is being perfected.

36. What else has to happen in order to guarantee to all human beings their true property and freedom?
Social wealth must not be acquired by individuals and left to chance – it must be managed and organized so that each gets apportioned his own.

37. According to which laws must social wealth be managed and the exchange of products conducted?
According to the laws of human nature and its needs.

38. Is it according to human nature that each man should be active in the same manner as the other, or that everyone should be always active in the same way?
On the contrary – it is according to human nature that the free activity or life enjoyment of one should not be like that of another, nor should it always be the same in the case of one person, but should be varied.

39. Is it according to human nature that all wealth should be equally distributed, so that all should receive the same means for their activity and their life?
On the contrary – it is according to human nature that the means for life or activity should be different, so that everyone will always receive those materials which he needs at any given time for his life activity.

40. Will no evil consequences follow from the fact that only freedom will determine activity?
When all men are humanely educated; when the special faculties of each person are developed; and finally, when everyone is offered the means for the application of his talents – then human society will have been organized according to the laws of its nature. Then it will become a living body, in which each part is fully developed in all directions and integrated organically with the whole so that it can carry out its function out of its inner living urges without need and coercion.

IV. Of the Transition to Communist Society

41. Can today's men establish immediately a communist society?
They can only introduce the preparations for a communist society.

42. Which preparations do we have to carry out?
Before everything else, we have to make contemporary society more conscious of its misery and its vocation for a better existence, so that the wish

for humane conditions – the wish to get out of the slavery in which we find ourselves – should be aroused in the majority of people. Next, when no power will be able to oppose any longer the success of the improvements, we shall have to abolish the needless state structures, which hold the powers of men hostage in the pay of despotism. Furthermore, taxes should be assessed in such a way that the greater the money wealth [of a person], the higher his taxes should be. Society should be in a position to call to life a truly humane, equal, universal, and free education, to buy up all the land, to set up large workshops and provide work for everyone who requires it: this could be achieved through savings in the existing expenditures, as well as through the rising income [of society] which would be achieved through a property tax, accompanied by essential changes in the law of inheritance.

43. Is it necessary to abolish the current property – money – through a decree?
It is neither necessary nor possible; the present property relations will be gradually transformed into communist forms once the steps just mentioned have been implemented. Money loses its value in the same measure as human beings gain in their worth. The worth of human beings rises towards infinity and the loss of value of money sinks into total worthlessness inasmuch as the organization of society is being established by its directing management and wage labour is being pushed aside; furthermore, [this is being enhanced] by the growth of the younger generation, which is already educated and brought up socially and carries out all these social kinds of labour. Once the measures mentioned here have been implemented, it would take at most one generation to remove the present property relations from society. On the other hand, a violent and sudden abolition of the current property relations would bear bad fruit. Rational property presupposes a rational society, and this in turn presupposes a socially educated human being, so that a sudden transformation of unorganic into organic property is unthinkable.

44. What changes have to be introduced to the laws of inheritance in the transition period?
Those who will be socially formed and educated [*gebildet*], as well as those who will enter into the new social organization, would not need inheritance; hence their inheritance reverts to society. Besides this, a general inheritance tax is to be introduced according to the principles of the property tax mentioned above.

45. Should one not fear an emigration of the wealthy, once this social reform is carried out?

One should not fear such an emigration. First of all, because in whatever country social reform starts, it will expand quickly all over the civilized world, so that the wealthy would be able to emigrate only to uncivilized nations; and for this they do not really have an inclination. Secondly, the measures that must be undertaken are not, according to our view, going to cause emigration among the wealthy people, since even a very high property tax would still leave them with the major part of their wealth. Thirdly, the representatives of the people could, if necessary, still undertake appropriate measures to prohibit such emigration or render it harmless. Finally, the damage that could be caused by the emigration of the capitalists will in any case be negligible; for as far as their personality is concerned, they are usually idle people; moreover, present society in any case does not suffer from scarcity of people but from surplus population. And as far as their wealth is concerned, at the utmost some metal money may be removed from society, which does not matter in any case, since true wealth will begin to replace false.

V. Of Matrimony

46. Does the current sexual relationship between man and woman accord with human nature?

It is according to human nature that a youngster loves a single girl and the girl a single youngster, and that as a rule they keep this exclusive relationship.

47. What is the cause of current unhappy marriages and debauchery in love?

They are caused by the violent oppression of love, which drives both sexes into inhuman, bestial, even towards unnatural debaucheries in love. Because of the property relations, which push woman into deepest misery and even force her to sell her body for money.

48. What bond should bind in a communist society man and wife in matrimony?

Mutual love.

49. What causes the dissolution of marriage?

It happens when mutual love does not exist any more.

50. Will no evil consequences follow for both sexes if love alone binds the matrimonial bond?

No evil consequences will follow from it, because human nature sinks to a bestial level only when it is being violently oppressed. Otherwise, as we said, marriage accords with human nature, and therefore true marriage will be attained only in the state of freedom, while at present it is only a cover for lechery. But the abuses, which appear now regarding property relations and the education of the young, cannot emerge in a society in which wealth and the education of the young are not left any longer to chance or the arbitrary will of the individual.

VI. Of Religion

51. Which religion should we all confess?

The religion of love and humanity.

52. Where is the testimony and proof for this religion?

In the hearts of all good people.

53. Is this universal human religion un-Christian?

No; it is rather a fulfilment of the Christian religion.

54. What is the goal of Christianity?

The salvation of all men through love, freedom, and justice.

55. Why has Christianity not yet reached its goal?

Because it has not yet clearly recognized what it truly is, and has not yet graphically imagined what it has wished for, believed in, and hoped for.

56. What is the belief of Christianity?

The belief in the bitter suffering of the human species [*Menschengattung*].

57. Under what image do Christian believers represent the human species?

Under the sign of the crucified Son of Man.

58. Is the belief of the Christians true?

It is true so long as the human species really suffers and in so far as one grasps the essentials of the Christian imagery.

59. May a Christian person hope that the suffering of mankind will cease one day?

Yes. This hope is even a part of his religion.

60. Under what sign does he imagine the better future of the human species?
Under the sign of heavenly joy in divine salvation. But we shall experience this heaven on earth when we no longer live in self-seeking and hate but in love, in a unified human species, in the communist society.

61. Are we evil by birth?
No, we become evil through the bad society in which we live.

62. Is Christian society, the Christian world, a bad one?
Yes, this world is, as Christianity itself attests, bad and abominable.

63. What is the name of the bad substance [*Wesen*] of this world, against which Christianity has always fulminated?
Its name is Money.

64. Is the Prince of the World, this Evil One or this Devil, against whose seduction Christianity warns us, essentially anything else than this con-founded Mammon, which we call our treasure?
No, it is nothing but the same. But Christians, who represent everything in graven images, have also imagined this confounded essence of money [*Geldwesen*] under the sign of the Devil.

65. Is hell anything else than this earth under the confounded dominion of money?
No, truly this earth is the actual, real hell.

66. Under what sign does Christianity imagine true, real life?
Under the sign of God in heaven.

67. Is God in heaven anything else than love?
No, it is the same.

68. What follows from love?
The whole creation, the whole universe, which is eternal, infinite, and immeasurable – just like love.

69. Is the creation something unchangeable, something that remains the same forever?
No, love constantly creates, and when it does not act any more, then everything is in a state of dissolution.

70. What is life?

It is love itself, which creates everything and makes its regeneration possible.

71. Is our God, in Whom we live and move [*leben und weben*] and wish to be, anything else than the human species or mankind as united in love?

No, it is the same.

72. Why have we believed until now that the Devil is in us, in the world, and that our God is not in us, not in the world, but in heaven?

Because until now we have not lived in our God, not in our species, not in love, but in alienation and enmity. Love has forsaken us and we were in the state of dissolution: hence we believed that our God was outside us and beyond this evil world, while the Devil was in us, in this world, in its very essence. As stated, our belief was not a fallacy: essentially, it was true. But once we unite and live in communism, hell will no longer be on earth and heaven will no longer be beyond this world; everything which has been presented to us by Christianity in prophecy and phantasy is about to be wholly realized in the true human society according to the eternal laws of love and reason.[1]

---

[1] In this last section of his *Credo*, Hess tries to present in simple language, supposedly accessible to a working-class reader or listener, the Spinozist ideas of immanence as if they were compatible with the Christian notion of the transcendence of God; he similarly tries to overcome the traditional Christian antinomy of belief and reason as if they were a seamless robe.

Consequences of a Revolution of the Proletariat

[First published in *Deutsche-Brüsseler-Zeitung* (German Brussels Gazette), 31 October 1847 (Second article).]

In order to be clear about the consequences of such a revolution, we should first acquaint ourselves with its pre-conditions. Let us then recapitulate them.

As we have seen, it is Big Industry which ultimately possesses all the means for the overthrow of the existing social organization that rests on private industry, private commerce, and private property. It is that which creates the revolutionary class and creates unity against the bourgeois class. It is that which makes it subjectively possible for the proletariat to cast off its yoke, by providing it with a consciousness of its situation. Finally, it is Big Industry which also brings about the objective material means for a social upheaval, by creating such a surplus of unutilized instruments of production that it is extremely easy to produce through them abundantly all that we require, once the obstacles which today hinder production at every turn are removed.

What is it which now hinders production? The commercial crises. How do these commercial crises arise? Through over-production. Why is more being produced today than can be consumed? Do all members of society possess a surplus of what they require? No: most do not have even the very necessities of life, much less all that a human being needs for the development of the totality of his inclinations, capacities, and powers; on the contrary, much more will have to be produced in order to satisfy all needs and the needs of all.

Why, then, is what is being produced today not being consumed? Whence this 'over-production', this surplus in the midst of shortage?

Well, as we have seen, the more progress private industry makes, the more private capital is concentrated in individual private hands, the more the propertyless are forced to sell their personal labour power to the property owners in order to acquire their most elementary means of livelihood. Yet the worker who is forced to sell himself – or what is the same, his labour power – becomes a commodity; his value follows the same economic laws as those of any other commodity. The progress of industry, the division of labour, the ever-developing instruments of production, the competition against machines as well as among the workers themselves – all these make the worker – as they make any other commodity – cheaper, and on average reduce his value to that of his costs of production, to the costs of his bare existence. Hence the worker cannot, on average, consume more than he needs for the continuation of his existence. He is not supposed to think of satisfying all his needs or to develop the totality of his inclinations, capacities, and powers.

But even he cannot at any given moment consume what he needs for the continuation of his existence. The economic law, according to which the prices of all commodities are reduced to their production costs, is – like every other economic law – right only generally or on average; in other words, it is an abstraction of reason. By comparing different cases and the fluctuations of the prices of commodities in the good and bad periods of commerce, we discover the general rule that these prices of commodities are calculated on average according to the costs necessary for their production. But private industry is in no way regulated by this law. So long as production is in the hands of private individuals, so long as exchange of products is similarly in private hands, one can never know how much or how little should be produced in order to satisfy the needs of consumers and not provide the world market with more or less goods than are being demanded or can be sold. This brings about the constant fluctuations in the prices of goods. Times of prosperity are followed by bad times, booms alternate with so-called commercial crises; regularly the latter follow the former.

Because private industry and private commerce cannot calculate the need of the world market, under our contemporary conditions production follows all kinds of omens and false symptoms. If goods are in demand on the world market, everyone seeks to exploit the boom as much as possible: production soars, buying is done on a speculative basis – i.e. one hopes to be able to re-sell the goods later with profit; eventually it becomes evident that the world market suffers from surfeit. Then everything becomes suddenly 'soft', as they say in business circles. Prices of goods fall below their cost of production; industrialists, who do not want to lose by continuing to produce, lay off workers. Consequently, the worker himself sinks below his costs of production, becomes 'soft'. No longer does he receive for his labour what he needs in order to exist. Hence a new cause for the diminution of consumption! The commercial crisis deepens, merchants fail, cannot hold out, go bankrupt. Less and less is being consumed, even less is being produced, as fear grips all industrialists and speculators. Due to lower production, the commercial crisis reaches its end. At last the world market shows a tendency for rising prices for goods; the few goods which are still around are being sold out. Once again the hope for profit smiles at the capitalists; once again, production is resumed.

What prospects open themselves to the worker, who is wrongly called a 'white slave' – he is not a slave, he is only a commodity; what prospects, do we ask, open themselves to this commodity? Well, its price too will recover; those workers, who have survived the crisis, who were not totally destroyed or have died during the crisis, their price rises as well. The consequence of this is that more workers are being produced, that the workers multiply – and one should remember that the workers multiply twofold: first, by not dying, marrying more, and having more children; secondly, because more middle-class people, who had been ruined during the crises, as well as agricultural or other workers, now flock to industrial or factory work. This competition, combined with the competition against machines, which are now daily being perfected and multiply, together with the increase in the division of labour and the transformation of handcraft into manufacture – all this, we say, once again depresses the value of the worker. To this should be added that the workers do not rise in price as quickly as other commodities, because unlike other commodities during the crisis not all of them have been consumed, but to a large extent they still exist – man is a tough being. The [price of the] worker does not therefore rise in the same measure in which it has sunk. Even under the best of circumstances, he rarely receives the [minimum] necessary for his own substance. The consumption of the mass of the people is thus continuously limited to certain simple victuals like, for example, bread, potatoes, alcohol, and to equally base clothes and woollens – victuals and clothes to which, by and large, production is also limited.

We have now seen what hinders production at present. It is not the lack of forces of production, it is the lack of purchasing power. The mass of the people is a commodity whose price, most of the time, is 'soft' and never rises much above its production costs. This is the reason why at present not more is consumed than can be produced, why production is limited both in its quality as well as quantity. Only when consumption rises can production be increased. Yet consumption cannot, in the long run, be increased, neither quantitatively nor qualitatively, let alone be improved, so long as the worker is a commodity, so long as his value is regulated by the economic laws of commodity prices. Only when the workers are no longer 'soft', will production cease to be 'soft', and all the needs of man, and the needs of all men, be richly satisfied.

Where should the workers start, so as not to be soft? Answer: they must cease to be a commodity, they must cease to sell themselves to Messrs Bourgeois. But what should they live on, after they cease to sell their labour in exchange for money to Messrs Bourgeois? What an extraordinary question! From what do Messrs Bourgeois themselves live? They live off their capital, from the profit and interest spewed by it. What is capital? Stored, accumulated labour. Have the owners of capital produced their own labour? No, they had the workers produce it on their account. Well, then! Will the workers not be able to produce for themselves what they can produce for Messrs Bourgeois for their account? No; in order to produce capital, one has to possess capital in one's own hands; one needs to have enough means of existence in stock, until one has created new means of existence through work; secondly, one needs to have the means for production, the instruments of production, the tools of labour. As everyone knows, the workers do not possess any capital, nor do they have sufficient means of existence during work at their disposal, even less so the tools of industry, least of all the instruments of production of big industry.

All, or nearly all, capital is in the hands of a few, in the hands of Messrs Bourgeois. Whence should then the workers get the capital which is needed to create capital? Yes, this is the Gordian knot which can be cut only by the sword! Out of their benevolence, Messrs Bourgeois will not let capital flow out of their hands for the benefit of the workers. Much as they praise the common weal, the welfare of the labouring class and repeat all other philanthropic turns of phrase, even the most philan-thropic bourgeois will not let themselves be moved in this direction! A revolution – this is the tacit condition which must precede this. One has to prove this to these gentlemen with striking arguments – because if the arguments are not *striking*, they prove nothing – one has to prove to them with striking arguments that they have to submit to the revolutionary measures which will be undertaken by a central administration set up by the workers.

These measures can be either directly aimed at achieving their goal – by transferring all instruments of production, including petty as well as big industries, into the hands of the workers for social production – or be of the kind that would lead to it gradually. It is unlikely that after a revolution one would immediately resort to direct measures, since in order to carry them out at least the majority of the whole people should agree to produce for the common account. Such an agreement could be assumed to exist at best among the workers of Big Industry, i.e. only among a part of the whole population.

On the other hand, there is no doubt that after the revolution of the proletariat those measures should be undertaken which are at present suggested by the democrats. These measures are:

Progressive taxation of the capitalists.

Partial or total abolition of the right of inheritance.

Expropriation of all princely, ecclesiastical, titled, and other estates, which would become ownerless through the revolution; the proceeds will be used for:

Establishment of large-scale common industrial or agricultural enterprises, which should be open to all who wish to work.

Establishment of national educational institutions, at which all youth will be educated, taught, and vocationally trained at the state's expense.

Supporting all sick people and those incapable of working. [1]

These measures are, by their nature, only transitory; they prepare a new social order and will recede into the background once the new social organization appears. They transform the present organization of society in a twofold manner, negative and positive; negatively, by undermining private industry; positively, by laying the foundations for a common industry, which entails completely new living and production relations from those of present society.

---

[1] These gradualist, yet at the same time radical, measures appear almost in identical form as the 'Ten Regulations' Marx and Engels suggest a year later for the first stage of the proletarian revolution in *The Communist Manifesto*; cf. Marx-Engels, *Selected Works*, I, pp. 53–4.

Even if only those ruined by competition join in the commonly owned industry, and even if for a short period after the revolution a not insignificant number of people would still be able to live off the interest or profit of their capital, in the long run no private industry will be able to survive once these measures are introduced. Nothing more is needed for the victory of commonly owned industry over private industry than the simple introduction of those measures now proposed by the radical democrats.

It has been said that state industry cannot compete with private industry. This is true only so long as private industry and private property are being protected by the state. Nowadays the state does not have the means to operate industry on a large scale, nor is private industry attacked at its root – capital – so that it would die from galloping consumption. Moreover, nowadays a state that would operate industry would find itself in an internal contradiction – both protecting private industry as well as competing with it; it further would be in conflict with public opinion, which would like to continue to maintain private property; finally, it would be in conflict with the interests of all those who do not belong to the state government or are state functionaries. This is so because so long as the state protects private industry and views itself as 'state' in contrast to 'civil society', its interests in no way merge with those of the people or of society. The interests of the government – be it as democratic in its origins, its principles, its inclinations as possible – would [still] be in conflict with the interests of the people, and its measures for the increase of the state's income through taxes, confiscation of property through any commercial or financial operation, would still be merely fiscal steps and would have economically no other meaning than [those measures undertaken] in Prussia or Russia, which by protecting private industry wish to maintain the present organization of society. In such a case, the measures suggested by the democrats would be far from being in the interest of the people or of progress: they would be a step backwards, in an economic as well as in a political sense. Instead of giving rise to the kind of self-government, self-rule, and self-administration advocated by all democrats – but never really achieved – they would merely establish a Russo-Turkish kind of government or, once it was clear that its measures and principles clashed with the interests of the people, they would be immediately retracted, thus bringing back to life – against their own intention – the old rule of the bourgeoisie, the old organization of society with its 'division of labour', with its free competition, with its proletariat and its misery.

The rule of the people [*Volksherrschaft*] and private industry are two irreconcilable contradictions, and nothing is more natural when one creates a state industry while letting private industry continue to exist than that the latter comes out triumphant and even puts constraints on the state industry, so that it can maintain its sickly existence only through emergency regulations and monopolies.

But once a government set up by the people openly declares war on private property in the interests of the people by establishing a massive national industry for the common account of all those who participate in it; once it provides itself with the means for the establishment of such a large-scale, common industry of the people [*Volksindustrie*] through progressive taxation of private property, limiting or abolishing the right of inheritance, and introducing other such measures which all attack private industry at its root by attacking capital; once it finally utilizes these means in order to develop all the capacities of the up-and-coming generation through public and free educational institutions, so that all youth will be able to apply its various inclinations and talents in a commonly owned industry – what future would private industry then have? It would lack everything it needs for its further existence: capital, men – both employers as well as workers – the means as well as the will.

Private property should not be attacked – neither by progressive taxes nor through the abolition of the right of inheritance – unless one wishes ultimately to abolish it; private industry should be safeguarded in its gains and be able to take pleasure in them if one wishes it to prosper. But can private industry take pleasure in its gains if even one of the measures advocated by the radical democrats is carried out?

We have seen that with the execution of those regulations one does not even need the bayonets of the proletariat for the defence of the commonly owned industry against the competition of private industry. Either these measures of the democrats will not be carried out, or all private industry, all private commerce, all private speculation – in one word: all private property – will be abolished once the institutions created by these democratic measures come into being.

These measures are, as we have said, only transitory, provisional, and revolutionary. Their positive part, public industry and education, is self-explanatory; it does not have to be propped up by any laws and decrees once its opposite – private industry and the lack of education of youth – becomes impossible; this part of the revolutionary measures becomes by itself a part of the whole organization of society. Its negative part, on the other hand – progressive taxation, limitations on the right of inheritance, and so on – disappears automatically once private property and inheritance cease to exist.

We see further that the 'split in the camp of the democrats', i.e. the conflict between the political democrats, socialists, labour organizers, etc., on the one hand, and communists on the other, exists only in the imagination of the former, but does not exist in reality once the measures proposed by the democrats themselves come into force – even if the socialists, democrats, and labour organizers shy away from their own measures once things start moving, so as not to pave the way for the communists. That, incidentally, these consequences look different in the minds of those socialists, democrats, and labour organizers from what they are in reality, is no more difficult to prove than discovering the illusions they have about their socialist, supposedly not communist, measures.

APPENDIX

Christ and Spinoza

(From *Rome and Jerusalem: The Last Nationality Question* [1862].)

In *Rome and Jerusalem* Hess articulated for the first time his project for the establishment of a Jewish socialist commonwealth in Palestine. Under the impact of the wars of Italian liberation and unification, Hess developed his view that human emancipation depends on a double path of liberation – social as well as national. He thus emphatically rejected his earlier views that the future of the Jews lies in integration into a radicalized revolutionary universalistic socialism, and his book is considered one of the first calls for what would later be called a Zionist approach to the future of the Jewish people.

While his political solution thus differs from that enunciated in his early writings, there is a continuity in his assessment of Spinoza, and also in the role he attributes to Jesus in world history. The following passages from *Rome and Jerusalem* attest to this aspect of continuity in Hess' thinking.

A Judaism reconciled with science [*Wissenschaft*] can do full justice to Christianity, fully acknowledge its world-historical significance, without falling into the pitfall of the shallow cosmopolitanism of the levelling tendencies of Reform Judaism, and without denying the character of Jewish religion. Today a Jewish historian does not need to relate fanatically or with indifference to a religion which is itself a product and consequently an essential component of Jewish history itself. The historian Graetz[1] solved

---

[1] Heinrich Graetz (1817–91), German Jewish historian, the founder of modern Jewish historiography. His eleven-volume *Geschichte der Juden*, published between 1853 and 1867, was the first modern attempt to present Jewish history as a national narrative, much under the

this problem in the third (actually the first) volume of his *Geschichte der Juden*, recently published in its second edition, showing how one can be at the same time a Jew – a pious, patriotic Jew – and an objective judge of that enormous phenomenon which has been for the Jews for eighteen centuries only a source of persecutions and oppressions . . .

The Jewish historian proves how following the Apostle Paul's joining the pagan views and life style, the first Christian community was riven by sectarian strife, whose traces can be found clearly in the various Gospels transmitted to us, the oldest of which were authored during the period of Bar-Kochba[2] (132–135 [AD]). In order to conquer the pagan world, the daughter of Judaism had to make as many concessions to paganism as the latter had to make to Judaism.

Christianity was a deviation, but a necessary deviation, from the classical essence of both Judaism and paganism. For Judaism, the world was and still is the holy product of a unified being. For paganism, in the classical appearance it had reached in Greece, the divine, harmonious unity was a product of the eternal representation of the manifold nature of the world.

The creative essence of Judaism did not go under with its classical creation, because the Jewish creator had not yet been absorbed in his creation. Classical paganism, on the other hand, saw its genius perish with its culture, whose roots lay on the surface of the ground which nourished it, and were swept away with the flood of nations which overtook it. To the pagans, who saw their own creative essence swept away with the ground on which it grew, the divine harmony of the manifold world, which they regarded as eternal, eventually appeared to them as devoid of divinity and depraved; and paganism sought refuge in the hereafter within the creative spirit of Judaism. On the other hand, the only Jews who could satisfy the religious needs of the pagans were those who became alienated from their own world, deserted Judaism, and had sunk themselves into the dying world of paganism in order to raise themselves out of it and with it towards the spirit which animated them – i.e. only such Jews who no more imagined the world as the holy product of a holy being, but as something sinful, deviating from God.

---

influence of Michelet and Ranke. It was translated into numerous languages, and became the main source of historical and cultural knowledge for modern educated Jews in Europe for many decades. While writing *Rome and Jerusalem* Hess was in close contact with Graetz, and he translated one volume of his opus into French.

[2] Shimon Bar-Kochba, the leader of the last Jewish insurrection in Palestine against the Romans during the time of Emperor Hadrian.

Thus the double Fall occurred – that of the profane from the divine and that of the divine from the profane – a world-less [*entweltlichtes*] Judaism within a godless paganism: the Christian world view of a Jewish saint, who became a pagan man in order to raise the nations towards the Spirit and prepare them for a future, better, divine world which was presented as that of the hereafter.

But in so far as in the course of the historical development the nations rose towards the Jewish religion of history, this hereafter [*Jenseits*] became more and more a here-and-now [*Diesseits*]. And the more the pagan world became more Jewish, i.e. more humanitarian, so too could the Jews participate in this culture which was progressing towards a better world. And finally, when after long battles between the pagan world view, sunk in raw sensuality and barbaric violence, and the Jewish world view which fled into a spiritualistic mysticism, the dawn of a modern, humanitarian civilization spread its mild rays in the Netherlandish republics over a better world, a Jew could give the signal that the spiritual development process of world-historical mankind has come to its end . . .

The teaching of Spinoza, the product of the Jewish genius and modern science [*Wissenschaft*], does not stand in contradiction with the Jewish teaching of unity – at most it may contradict its rationalistic and supernaturalistic approach. What is stressed by Jewish revelation since Moses is not transcendence as an opposition to immanence, but unity as against the multiplicity of the creative being. This was expressed long ago before the destruction of the Second Temple by the Jewish philosopher Philo,[3] later repeated in the Middle Ages by the great Jewish philosophers of religion of the Spanish cultural period and finally, in the modern age, expressed again by Spinoza with all the sharpness and depth of his spiritual genius.

It is obvious why uncritical dogmatism, which discerns in the oriental images of the holy language a mass of dogmas, sets against Spinozism the dead letter of the Bible and damns the immanent knowledge of God as heresy. The rationalists, on the other hand, who interpret all anthropomorphisms arbitrarily, do not have the slightest basis in the Bible for putting up their theory as against that of Spinoza.

Neither in heaven, nor in a distant place, should one, according to Moses, seek the teaching of God: rather He reveals Himself in ourselves,

---

[3] Philo was a Jewish Hellenistic first-century philosopher from Alexandria (Egypt), who tried to combine his Jewish faith with the tenets of classical Greek philosophy; hence he later became a model for Jewish thinkers like Maimonides and Spinoza whose philosophical projects have tried, in different ways, to combine both traditions.

in our spirit and heart. It is for this reason that the Talmud maintains, probably in contradiction to some sayings in the Torah (which maintained, among others, that the glory of God descended down to earth) that, on the contrary, 'never has the Godhead [*shechina*] descended to earth and never did Moses ascend to the heavens'. The all-presence of God makes any spatial and temporal movement from Him to us, as well as from us to Him, appear at least as superfluous . . .

An other-worldly [*jenseitiger*] God, who does not relate to man as permanently present creator and revelation, is neither the God of the Jews nor the Christians nor the Mohammedans . . .

Index

Index

CAMBRIDGE TEXTS IN THE
HISTORY OF POLITICAL THOUGHT

Diderot *Political Writings* (edited by John Hope Mason and Robert Wokler)
0 521 36911 8 paperback

The Dutch Revolt (edited by Martin van Gelderen)
0 521 39809 6 paperback

Early Greek Political Thought from Homer to the Sophists (edited by Michael Gagarin and Paul Woodruff)
0 521 43768 7 paperback

The Early Political Writings of the German Romantics (edited by Frederick C. Beiser)
0 521 44951 0 paperback

The English Levellers (edited by Andrew Sharp)
0 521 62511 4 paperback

Erasmus *The Education of a Christian Prince* (edited by Lisa Jardine)
0 521 58811 1 paperback

Fenelon *Telemachus* (edited by Patrick Riley)
0 521 45662 2 paperback

Ferguson *An Essay on the History of Civil Society* (edited by Fania Oz-Salzberger)
0 521 44736 4 paperback

Filmer *Patriarcha and Other Writings* (edited by Johann P. Sommerville)
0 521 39903 3 paperback

Fletcher *Political Works* (edited by John Robertson)
0 521 43994 9 paperback

Sir John Fortescue *On the Laws and Governance of England* (edited by Shelley Lockwood)
0 521 58996 7 paperback

Fourier *The Theory of the Four Movements* (edited by Gareth Stedman Jones and Ian Patterson)
0 521 35693 8 paperback

Franklin *The Autobiography and Other Writings on Politics, Economics, and Virtue* (edited by Alan Houston)
0 521 54265 0 paperback

Gramsci *Pre-Prison Writings* (edited by Richard Bellamy)
0 521 42307 4 paperback

Guicciardini *Dialogue on the Government of Florence* (edited by Alison Brown)
0 521 45623 1 paperback

Hamilton, Madison, and Jay (writing as 'Publius') *The Federalist* with *The Letters of 'Brutus'* (edited by Terence Ball)
0 521 00121 8 paperback

Harrington *A Commonwealth of Oceana* and *A System of Politics* (edited by J. G. A. Pocock)
0 521 42329 5 paperback

Hegel *Elements of the Philosophy of Right* (edited by Allen W. Wood and H. B. Nisbet)
0 521 34888 9 paperback

Hegel *Political Writings* (edited by Laurence Dickey and H. B. Nisbet)
0 521 45979 3 paperback

Hess *The Holy History of Mankind and Other Writings* (edited by Shlomo Avineri)
0 521 38756 6 paperback

Hobbes *On the Citizen* (edited by Michael Silverthorne and Richard Tuck)
0 521 43780 6 paperback

Hobbes *Leviathan* (edited by Richard Tuck)
0 521 56797 1 paperback

Hobhouse *Liberalism and Other Writings* (edited by James Meadowcroft)
0 521 43726 1 paperback

Hooker *Of the Laws of Ecclesiastical Polity* (edited by A. S. McGrade)
0 521 37908 3 paperback

Hume *Political Essays* (edited by Knud Haakonssen)
0 521 46639 3 paperback

King James VI and I *Political Writings* (edited by Johann P. Sommerville)
0 521 44729 1 paperback

Jefferson *Political Writings* (edited by Joyce Appleby and Terence Ball)
0 521 64841 6 paperback

John of Salisbury *Policraticus* (edited by Cary Nederman)
0 521 36701 8 paperback

Kant *Political Writings* (edited by H. S. Reiss and H. B. Nisbet)
0 521 39837 1 paperback

Knox *On Rebellion* (edited by Roger A. Mason)
0 521 39988 2 paperback

Kropotkin *The Conquest of Bread and Other Writings* (edited by Marshall Shatz)
0 521 45990 7 paperback

Lawson *Politica sacra et civilis* (edited by Conal Condren)
0 521 39248 9 paperback

Leibniz *Political Writings* (edited by Patrick Riley)
0 521 35899 X paperback

The Levellers (edited by Andrew Sharp)
0 521 62511 4 paperback

Locke *Political Essays* (edited by Mark Goldie)
0 521 47861 8 paperback

Locke *Two Treatises of Government* (edited by Peter Laslett)
0 521 35730 6 paperback

Loyseau *A Treatise of Orders and Plain Dignities* (edited by Howell A. Lloyd)
0 521 45624 X paperback

Luther and Calvin on Secular Authority (edited by Harro Höpfl)
0 521 34986 9 paperback

Machiavelli *The Prince* (edited by Quentin Skinner and Russell Price)
0 521 34993 1 paperback

de Maistre *Considerations on France* (edited by Isaiah Berlin and Richard Lebrun)
0 521 46628 8 paperback

Maitland *State, Trust and Corporation* (edited by David Runciman and Magnus Ryan)
0 521 52630 2 paperback

Malthus *An Essay on the Principle of Population* (edited by Donald Winch)
0 521 42972 2 paperback

Proudhon *What is Property?* (edited by Donald R. Kelley and Bonnie G. Smith)
0 521 40556 4 paperback

Pufendorf *On the Duty of Man and Citizen according to Natural Law* (edited by James Tully)
0 521 35980 5 paperback

The Radical Reformation (edited by Michael G. Baylor)
0 521 37948 2 paperback

Rousseau *The Discourses and Other Early Political Writings* (edited by Victor Gourevitch)
0 521 42445 3 paperback

Rousseau *The Social Contract and Other Later Political Writings* (edited by Victor Gourevitch)
0 521 42446 1 paperback

Seneca *Moral and Political Essays* (edited by John Cooper and John Procope)
0 521 34818 8 paperback

Sidney *Court Maxims* (edited by Hans W. Blom, Eco Haitsma Mulier, and Ronald Janse)
0 521 46736 5 paperback

Sorel *Reflections on Violence* (edited by Jeremy Jennings)
0 521 55910 3 paperback

Spencer *The Man versus the State* and *The Proper Sphere of Government* (edited by John Offer)
0 521 43740 7 paperback

Stirner *The Ego and Its Own* (edited by David Leopold)
0 521 45647 9 paperback

Thoreau *Political Writings* (edited by Nancy Rosenblum)
0 521 47675 5 paperback

Tonnies *Community and Civil Society* (edited by Jose Harris and Margaret Hollis)
0 521 56119 1 paperback

Utopias of the British Enlightenment (edited by Gregory Claeys)
0 521 45590 1 paperback

Vico *The First New Science* (edited by Leon Pompa)
0 521 38726 4 paperback

Vitoria *Political Writings* (edited by Anthony Pagden and Jeremy Lawrance)
0 521 36714 x paperback

Voltaire *Political Writings* (edited by David Williams)
0 521 43727 x paperback

Weber *Political Writings* (edited by Peter Lassman and Ronald Speirs)
0 521 39719 7 paperback

William of Ockham *A Short Discourse on Tyrannical Government* (edited by A. S. McGrade and John Kilcullen)
0 521 35803 5 paperback

William of Ockham *A Letter to the Friars Minor and Other Writings* (edited by A. S. McGrade and John Kilcullen)
0 521 35804 3 paperback

Wollstonecraft *A Vindication of the Rights of Men* and *A Vindication of the Rights of Woman* (edited by Sylvana Tomaselli)
0 521 43633 8 paperback

Printed in Great Britain
by Amazon

67944910R00112